THE SEVEN BIG MYTHS
ABOUT
MARRIAGE

THE SEVEN BIG MYTHS ABOUT MARRIAGE

*What Science, Faith, and Philosophy
Teach Us about Love and Happiness*

By
Christopher Kaczor with Jennifer Kaczor

IGNATIUS PRESS   SAN FRANCISCO

Cover photograph © iStockPhoto.com

Cover design by John Herreid

© 2014 by Ignatius Press, San Francisco
ISBN 978-1-58617-843-7
Library of Congress Control Number 2013916524
Printed in the United States of America ∞

FOR SUSAN AND STEVE SENIA

thank you, thank you, thank you

CONTENTS

Happiness and Identity

My wife Jennifer likes to keep it real:

> My husband and I were a little late to the home-buying party. Specifically, we had been married for almost twenty years when we could finally, kind of, sort of, if we stopped feeding the kids, afford to buy a house. And so we did. We took everything we had, quite of bit of what other people had, and a lot of what the government promised, and we bought a house. I wish we had not. The list of things I am not allowed to buy anymore is overwhelming in its detail and its scope. It starts with clothes and haircuts, and ends in the emergency room. I do have enough premium denim to last me a good solid year, and with spring on the way I can count on Mother Nature to help me in the highlights department. I am not looking for sympathy on those accounts. This weekend I cut fourteen-year-old Caroline's hair (she cried for only a few hours afterward), and I now buzz the boys' hair myself.
>
> But it gets worse. "No more fast food", my husband informed me. "Even when I'm running kids between two, three, four different athletic events?" I whined. "Nope", he said. "Plan ahead." Darn. Okay, fast food

is bad for the kids anyway, and if I cannot slap together a few PB&J sandwiches at this point in my career, I cannot really call myself a mother. Fine. I'll live.

Now, I realize, reader, that if you have stayed with me this far, you are beginning to be disgusted. "This woman is a baby", you are thinking. "Fast food and premium demin?" you are muttering to yourself. "There are some folks in Haiti that I would like to introduce her to." Yes, yes, I know. I myself am somewhat embarrassed. But two things, reader, two things. First, it gets worse. Stay with me. Second—and you are not going to like this—I challenge you to give your spending a once-over and see how you rate. I am not going to push; I am just saying ... People spend thousands on quack nutritionists, and I do not see anyone attacking them. Apparently, paying some weirdo to diagnose imaginary digestive problems is fine, but wanting to look your best in the latest fashions is hedonistic.

Anyway, when we still could not make ends meet with the peanut butter and jelly, my husband informed me, by way of turning off my reading light, that we would be giving up electricity. "What!" I bellowed. "I am the only mother *anywhere* in America who doesn't own a cell phone, and now I have to give up reading!" "Just for a year or so," he said, "until my income increases." "Well ... urrgh", I said to the dark form next to me.

In the morning, by way of natural light, I resumed my reading. It is like living in Bill Gates' opposite world. I read somewhere that his house is so smart that as his lovely wife moves from room to room, her music, lighting, and television move from room to room with her. Not only is my house not as smart as Bill Gates', but neither is my husband. First, he does not wait until I leave a room to turn off the light, preferring, instead, to flip the switch in anticipation of my leaving the room at some theoretical time in the future. "I'm tying my shoes!" I scream from behind the wardrobe, only to hear back, "Wear slip-ons." But one night we reached an apex, and I think I made my point. As I was cautiously feeling my way down a pitch-black hallway, I stumbled over a folded mat and went head over heels, landing on my you-know-what. "Ow!" I screamed. "This has to stop!" Chris and the kids felt their way through their various dark rooms until they found me in the hallway. Risking foreclosure, Chris turned on the light and helped me up. "The idea", he said, "is that you turn on the light when you enter a room, and turn it off when you leave. The math is really very simple."

"Yes, it is", I said. "Even a straightforward divorce is expensive, but one complicated by negligent injury claims could cost you the house." And then, of course, because he is such a good man and takes such good care of our family, I apologized, turned off the light, and lightly kissed him while the kids all yelled, "Eww!"

The gritty, nonglamorous, everyday reality of marriage is known only once one has become married—indeed, only once one has been married for a while. It is that reality that my wife Jennifer captures so well.

But how did this all begin? Let me recall another memory. The year was 1992, and I was at Saint James Cathedral in Seattle. The tuxedo fit fine, but the rented shoes were a little big. I stood in front of the altar, and next to me stood a stunning woman in a white dress. My five closest guy friends were on my right. Her five closest girlfriends were on her left. In the middle, before us, was a priest, the pastor of the cathedral, Father Michael G. Ryan, whom I had known since childhood. Along with 350 of our friends and family, he would witness the most important commitment I would ever make. I tried to stand up as straight as I could, for I knew that everyone in the place was looking at and listening to me. Taking Jennifer's hands in mine, I spoke loudly and clearly, "I, Christopher, take you, Jennifer, to be my wife. I promise to be true to you in good times and in bad, in sickness and in health, until death do us part. I will love you and honor you all the days of my life." After a moment of silence, she, in a softer voice, said to me, "I, Jennifer, take you, Christopher, to be my husband. I promise to be true to you in good times and in bad, in sickness and in health, until death do us part. I will love you and honor you all the days of my life."

What my wife and I did on that day, I had seen done countless times before in movies and in reality. In exchanging vows, we had done what our parents and grandparents had done, following innumerable generations before. In taking the vows, we became husband and wife; we were married. Although I knew something about the nature of marriage, I did not realize at twenty-two how much more I had to learn. Although I now realize how much more I still have to learn, in this book, I write about what I wish I had known—or had known more clearly—on that bright day in 1992.

One of the most important things that I learned was the nature of happiness. Indeed, I think that without a sound understanding of what happiness is, a person will be frustrated in finding happiness whether or not he is married. We all want to be happy. Every day, in whatever we do, we seek this goal—one that we share with every other person on the planet. Many people seek marriage because they believe that marriage or their spouse will make them happy. But will it?

To answer this question, it is necessary to examine happiness. What exactly is happiness? How can we find it? What really helps us to become happy, and what does not matter much at all? The answers that we give to these questions make a great deal of difference for our vision of what marriage is. Indeed, the way we live our lives answers these questions and determines the kinds of persons we become.

The Hedonist, the Egoist, the Altruist, and the Altruist of Faith

Different kinds of people seek happiness in different ways. Robert J. Spitzer, S.J., in his book *Healing the Culture*, distinguishes four different kinds of activities that people do in seeking happiness.[1] The hedonist seeks happiness in bodily pleasure obtained by food, drink, drugs, or sex. The hedonist seeks what Spitzer calls level one happiness. The egoist seeks happiness in competitive advantage over other people in terms of money, fame, power, popularity, or

[1] Robert J. Spitzer, *Healing the Culture* (San Francisco: Ignatius Press, 2000).

other material goods. This Spitzer calls level two happiness. At level three, the altruist seeks happiness through loving and serving other people. And at level four, the altruist of faith, or the spiritual altruist, seeks happiness in loving and serving God and the image of God found in every human person.

We can group the hedonist and the egoist together. They are two varieties of fundamentally selfish persons. We can also group the altruist and the altruist of faith together. They are two kinds of generous, loving persons. Indeed, the altruist or altruist of faith is not just a good person but an excellent person.

Many people think about ethics as primarily a matter of obeying rules or of making the world a better place. Rules and consequences of action both have their due place. But ethics is primarily about becoming a particular kind of person, hopefully a loving, excellent person. Indeed, we are becoming a different person each day. Each choice is self-shaping, transforming us into a particular kind of person—a hedonist, an egoist, an altruist, or a spiritual altruist. Each choice moves us toward becoming an ideally loving person or toward becoming a fully selfish person. Ethics is about *identity*, who we are now and who we are becoming.

Each one of us is a potential hedonist, egoist, altruist, or spiritual altruist. What we choose determines what kind of person we become. Although most people desire each level of happiness at different times and in different ways, not every level provides equal and lasting contentment.

In life, we are constantly faced with choosing between one level of happiness and another. For example, the Olympic athlete seeking victory chooses success in athletics over pleasures of the body found in abusing drugs or alcohol. The businessperson gains level one happiness by sleeping in late on Monday morning, but this choice sacrifices level two happiness in terms of advancing a career. Since we often have to choose one activity over another, and since sometimes choosing one level of happiness undermines another level of happiness, it makes sense to think through what kinds of activities will truly lead to lasting joy.

The Happiness of the Hedonist: Level One

The happiness of the hedonist, which comes from seeking bodily pleasures, has several advantages. It is easy to get, it arrives fairly quickly, and it can be intense. For example, it is easy to drink beer; drinkers can feel the effects of alcohol within minutes; and intoxication is, well, intoxicating. Every baby begins life as a little hedonist devoted exclusively to level one happiness—seeking the pleasures brought by milk, and avoiding the pain brought by hunger and a dirty diaper. The infant has no understanding of or desire for the higher levels of happiness but seeks simple bodily comfort.

Everyone desires level one happiness, but the hedonist tries to become satisfied with level one happiness alone or in preference to the higher levels of happiness. Aside from infants and hard-core drug addicts, almost all human beings seek deeper levels of happiness. We realize that we want more, in part because of the many inherent difficulties associated with devotion to bodily pleasure.

One difficulty with the happiness of the hedonist is that it leaves almost as quickly as it arrives. When we are hungry, nothing sounds better than a warm, filling meal. But when dinner is over, the pleasures of satiating hunger are also over. The pleasures of the body arise quickly, but these pleasures also depart quickly.

A second weakness of seeking happiness in bodily pleasures—at least those of drink, drugs, and sex—is that we build a tolerance to the things that bring us this level of happiness, so that more is needed to achieve the same degree of enjoyment. I remember vividly the first time I drank alcohol with my friend Kinnon. We had a six-pack of malt liquor. Before we had finished splitting the beer, I was in another world, a very pleasant world. After starting to drink regularly, I discovered that the amount of alcohol that had previously led to a pleasurable buzz no longer got me to the same level of enjoyment. I quickly built up a tolerance. The more I drank, the greater the tolerance I developed and the more I needed to drink to achieve the same amount of level one happiness. The hedonist finds himself with increasingly great desires that become increasingly difficult to satisfy. In the case of alcohol and drug abuse, this can lead to fatal consequences.

Centuries ago, the philosopher Plato, in his dialogue *Gorgias*, illustrated the way in which we grow to need greater doses of level one happiness. Level one contentment is like filling up a pitcher to the rim. As you fill up the pitcher with bodily pleasure, over time it begins to spring leaks. So, to continue to fill it up to the rim, you must pour in still more. As you fill it up more often, even more leaks spring in the pitcher—and the more difficult the job of finding satisfaction becomes as the leaks multiply. Devotion to level one happiness is like feeding a stray cat in your backyard. The feral cat calls for food, so you feed it. The cat is happy, and so are you. The next day it calls for food again and brings along a couple of its friends, and since the hungry cats are calling loudly, you feed them again. As the days progress, the number of cats multiplies until you are overwhelmed. The way to stop the ever-increasing number of strays surrounding your house is to stop feeding the stray cats. The more you feed them, the more numerous they will become. Plato captured what I and countless others have experienced: Seeking bodily pleasure as the aim of life becomes a self-defeating goal.

Addiction, and its devastating consequences, is yet another crisis of level one happiness. Hedonists discover that the pleasures of food, drink, drugs, and sex can lead to obsession and compulsion. As the addict and those around the addict realize, to the great pain of all involved, the addict's enslavement is the opposite of real happiness. Indeed, for many addicts, the intense cravings for their "high" undermine their integrity, demolish their future plans, and devastate their relationships. Compulsive level one behavior leaves the addict alone, depressed, over-whelmed, hopeless, and in despair of ever living a clean, sober, and free life. Level one happiness can become level one misery.

Even if one never becomes an addict, disordered devotion to level one happiness is superficial and eventually boring. We all want bodily pleasure, but almost all of us also want to achieve something more meaningful and important in life. Imagine, for example, that scientists develop an "experience machine".[2] When you enter

---

[2] Robert Nozick, *Anarchy, State, and Utopia* (Oxford: Blackwell, 1974), 42–45; Germain Grisez and Russell Shaw, *Beyond the New Morality* (Notre Dame, Ind.: University of Notre Dame Press, 1974), 26.

this device, the scientists stimulate your brain so that you experience intense bodily pleasure such as arises from sex, drugs, alcohol, and food. Now suppose that the scientists approach you with this proposition: "In this machine, we can stimulate your brain to feel the most intense bodily pleasure possible, and we can also feed you through a tube in your stomach and take care of your other bodily needs. But once you enter the machine, you must remain permanently within it, forever attached and within the confines of the control booth. At the expiration of your natural life, which we expect to be around eighty years of age, we will remove your corpse from the box and dispose of it however you like. Would you like to enter the pleasure machine permanently right now?"

I am guessing that you would answer, "No, thank you. No permanent pleasure box for me." We want real life, real friends, and real experiences. We want what the pleasure machine cannot give us. We want *actually* to do certain things, not just have the mirage of doing them without the reality. We want to grow stronger and develop our powers and possibilities rather than just be an indeterminate blob experiencing nothing real and stuck in a machine. We want actual contact with reality, not just a ceaseless artificial evasion of real life. We want higher levels of happiness that are not possible in bodily pleasure alone.

For reasons such as these, almost all human beings move beyond exclusive devotion to level one happiness. As mentioned earlier, only babies and hard-core addicts are dominated exclusively by level one concerns. Virtually everyone moves beyond being a mere hedonist. When level one happiness and the higher levels of happiness come into conflict, almost everyone, more or less regularly, chooses the higher levels of happiness.

The Happiness of the Egoist: Level Two

The egoist has moved beyond the hedonist and seeks happiness that has greater meaning and significance than that of level one. The level two happiness of the egoist consists of "winning" at some competition. The egoist wants not merely to keep up with the Joneses but to surpass them— in money, fame, popularity, or status. At this level, we seek happiness through victory in whatever "game" we choose to play. It could involve material possessions—"He who dies with the most toys wins." It could involve advancement in a chosen field, such as becoming the CEO, the league champion, or the prima ballerina. It could involve that social victory of dating the football quarterback or the homecoming queen. It could involve achieving the highest score on the exam, purchasing the newest car, or wearing the latest fashions to impress others.

The level two happiness of the egoist has several advantages over the level one happiness of the hedonist. Although level one happiness is easier to obtain, level two happiness tends to last longer. We can bask in the afterglow of victory for weeks. Another advantage of the happiness of the egoist over that of the hedonist is that there are no physical addictions associated with level two happiness. Furthermore, as a culture, we celebrate level two achievements— at graduation, we recognize the valedictorian and the top student athlete, but no awards are given for whoever drank the most beer or hooked up with the most people.

However, will the egoist be able to enjoy lasting happiness? By way of example, we could focus on level two in terms of fame, popularity, or power. But perhaps the most common way people seek level two happiness is through money. Many people believe and act as if the good life—the happy life—can be found through having money, spending money, or both. But can we find lasting happiness in large salaries and lavish spending, in producing and consuming?

Scientists have studied this question extensively.[3] It turns out that more money can make you much happier—if you live in abject poverty. If you do not have clothes to keep you warm, if you have no food for your children and no roof over your head, then money for these basic provisions greatly improves reported happiness. However, once you have enough money for food, clothing, and shelter, increases in money are unrelated to stable increases in happiness. When researchers compared people with annual incomes of $30,000, $100,000, and $500,000, they found little difference in self-reported happiness or levels of depression.

So victory over others in terms of money will not satisfy the egoist. But what about other ways the egoist might try to find happiness aside from through money? No matter what the arena of competition (money, power, fame, social status), the egoist will never be lastingly satisfied with winning, no matter how great the victory. A musician might think, "If I could just have my own album, that would

<hr />

[3] For a wonderful summary of this research, see David G. Meyers, "Will Money Buy Happiness?" in *Positive Psychology: Exploring the Best in People*, ed. Shane J. Lopez (Westport, Conn.: Praeger, 2008), 4:35–56.

be such an amazing achievement that I would certainly be happy." After his first album appears, the musician is delighted, but over time the glow of seeing it for sale fades. The musician might then think, "If I could have the best-selling album of the year, then I would achieve lasting happiness." If he achieves this goal, he would probably be quite happy for a while, but before long, some other artist would take his place, and he would find himself dissatisfied. Finally, he might say, "Well, if I had the best-selling album of all time, then I would achieve lasting happiness."

Michael Jackson was in this very position. His 1983 album *Thriller* is the best-selling album of all time, garnering more than double the sales of the second-best-selling album. But after demolishing the competition, was the King of Pop satisfied?

It certainly does not seem so. Following *Thriller*, Jackson said he spent the rest of his life trying to make an album that would outsell *Thriller*.[4] Being number one was not good enough, even for the person who was number one. As Bertrand Russell put it, "Napolean envied Caesar, Caesar envied Alexander, and Alexander, I daresay, envied Hercules, who never existed. You cannot, therefore, get away from envy by means of success alone, for there will always be in history or legend some person even more successful than you are."[5]

The final and perhaps most obvious examples of the failure of the hedonist and the egoist to find lasting happiness

[4]Nancy Griffin, "The 'Thriller' Diaries", *Vanity Fair*, July 2010, http://www.vanityfair.com/hollywood/features/2010/07/michael-jackson-thriller-201007.

[5]Bertrand Russell, quoted in Meyers, "Will Money Buy Happiness?", 49.

are the lives of celebrities. Celebrities have more alcohol than they can drink, more drugs than they can take (and still remain alive), and more willing, attractive potential partners than there is time in the day to have sex. They can, and often do, "max out" in terms of the happiness of the hedonist. In terms of egoist happiness, celebrities have money enough for palatial residences in Malibu and in Manhattan, the power to make or break people's careers, popularity such that millions of people read magazines to learn the minutiae of their lives, and fame so great that they can walk into any bar and everyone knows their name.

But what do maximum level one and maximum level two bring to celebrities? Many of them are apparently so deliriously happy that they end up committing suicide. Other celebrities teeter on the brink of self-inflicted death through drug and alcohol abuse. Many celebrities end up not with deep happiness but with divorce, legal action, and rehabilitation. The crash-and-burn examples of countless celebrities make abundantly clear the point made by Aristotle and Aquinas centuries ago. Happiness cannot be found in bodily pleasure, money, fame, popularity, or power. Level one and level two happiness, even in superabundant celebrity doses, cannot deliver happiness. The happiness of the hedonist and the egoist combined and maximized does not produce lasting happiness.

The discussion thus far has focused on the "winners" of level two. But of course, it is overwhelmingly unlikely that we will ever have the recording success of Michael Jackson, the fame of Marilyn Monroe, or the money of a Hollywood mogul. If even *winning* at level two does not satisfy, how much more does *losing* at level two fail to satisfy? If we think that our happiness, our self-worth, and our basic meaning in life are found in being an egoist, then we risk finding ourselves as losers in the level two competition. As level two losers, we will be depressed, consider ourselves worthless, and believe that life is not worth living. Level two "winners" really do not win, and level two "losers" do no better in terms of happiness—in fact, they probably do worse.

Egoism cannot satisfy us in part because the friendships and intimate relationships of those at level two—whether winners or losers—suffer from a focus on the negative.

Level two is inherently about comparison with others, and the egoist is always keeping score. He is especially anxious to find the "bad news" in other people so as to make himself superior by comparison. This focus on what is wrong with others is not simply a matter of noticing the negative; this cannot be helped and is needed for a realistic understanding of other people. Rather, the egoist goes beyond merely noticing the negatives of other people and focuses upon them, relishes them, and defines other persons in terms of them.

Why? Well, the egoist gets ahead in level two in part by dragging other people down. The worse the other people are, the better the egoist seems by comparison. The losers of level two are eager to expose the weaknesses of the level two winners. The winners look for what is wrong with the losers to emphasize their superiority. For egoists, this negative perspective on others is habitual. As Abraham Lincoln noted, "Those who look for the bad in people will surely find it." But we can also choose to look for the good in ourselves and in others in order to become happier. We can begin, in short, to find happiness at deeper levels.

The Happiness of the Altruist: Level Three

To be an altruist is to love human persons and in this love to find happiness. To love someone always involves three elements: (1) willing what is good for the person loved, (2) an appreciation for the person loved, and (3) a desire for unity with the person loved.[6] Level three happiness does not necessarily contradict or undermine success at level two or enjoyment of level one, but it prioritizes love and service to others over self-aggrandizement and self-indulgence.

Nothing is inherently wrong with worldly success or with bodily pleasures. The trouble comes when self-aggrandizement and self-indulgence are the ultimate goal of life; when we subordinate more important things (level three and level four happiness) to less important things (level one and level two happiness); and when we choose the lesser levels of happiness in a way that damages the higher levels of happiness. As isolated and suicidal

---

[6] Alexander Pruss, *One Body: An Essay in Christian Sexual Ethics* (Notre Dame, Ind.: University of Notre Dame Press, 2012). This is a truly excellent scholarly treatment of the most fundamental questions in Christian sexual ethics. Altruists are sometimes viewed as caring for the other without any self-regard whatsoever. I am using the term "altruist" as a synonym for a person animated by *agape*. The one who has agape seeks the good of both people, a joint good. As Pruss puts it, "The lover seeks union, but seeks a union that is essentially a joint good. This joint good is good not only for the lover but also for the beloved, and insofar as this love is not, say, lust, it is sought as a joint good. Thus, the lover does not seek his or her own good, but the joint good of lover and beloved" (15).

celebrities make clear, we cannot be happy without true friendship and true love, and we cannot have true friendship and true love without acting in ways that accord with friendship and love.

In willing what is good for the beloved, the altruist seeks to serve people and therefore also rejects actions that intentionally undermine the well-being of people, such as murder, theft, perjury, lies, assault, insults, malicious gossip, and harassment. An altruist does not destroy or endanger the well-being of others without good reason, because he seeks to enhance the well-being of others. An altruist who does a selfish action—that is, who chooses level one or two happiness at the expense of level three or four happiness—is not only acting inconsistently with his identity but is no longer acting as an altruist.

Although people living at level three still want level one and level two happiness, they are willing to give up these lower pleasures if they interfere with or undermine those of level three. So, although many altruists would like to have more money, they choose not to steal, since theft enhances level two but only at the cost of level three. Although they may enjoy drinking alcohol, generous people choose not to drive after drinking, since this undermines level three happiness by endangering other people. (The generous person who does drink and drive is not acting in this instance as a generous person but is contradicting his identity as an altruist and is changing himself into a selfish person.) Excellent people certainly enjoy both bodily pleasure and success in competition, but they do not enjoy pleasure or success when these are accomplished at the expense of love of neighbor. From a level three (and level four) perspective, love is the measure of whether an action is right or wrong, and people who love choose what is truly good and avoid what is bad.

The happiness of the altruist is deeply meaningful because his point is to enrich the lives of other people. Although level three happiness takes more effort than that of level one, it tends to last longer. In fact, people tend to overestimate how much pleasure level one will bring and tend to underestimate the longer-lasting happiness of level three activities. Martin Seligman, former president of the American Psychological Association and founder of positive psychology, has noted that when people compare fun to philanthropy they find, often to their surprise, that the philanthropic activities provide greater and more lasting joy.[7]

In addition to joy, another key characteristic of the altruist is looking for the good news in others, an appreciation of the person loved. Every person on earth has strengths and good qualities as well as weaknesses. No one is perfectly good; no one is perfectly bad. The altruist focuses on what is good, on what is positive, and on what potential could be developed. By contrast, the hedonist and the egoist view other people as stepping-stones on the way to greater pleasure, wealth, popularity, power, fame, or victory. The selfish person uses other people to enjoy level one pleasure or level two success.

The positive orientation of the altruist, as you might imagine, enhances human relationships. Researchers in marital and family therapy talk about the "magic ratio" of

[7] Martin E. P. Seligman, *Authentic Happiness: Using the New Positive Psychology to Realize Your Potential for Lasting Fulfillment* (New York: Free Press, 2003), 9.

positive interactions to negative interactions.[8] In healthy relationships, there are about five positive interactions, comments, and acts to every one negative interaction. When the ratio of positive to negative dips below this level, the relationship turns bitter or ends.

Finally, the altruist finds happiness in being united with people. The altruist seeks to join with others in various activities to further human well-being. The form that this unity takes depends upon the reality of the loved person and the relationship that exists. The kind of unity a husband and wife enjoy differs from the kind of unity it is appropriate for siblings and mere friends to enjoy. The union of love takes various forms, but love always seeks some kind of appropriate union with the one who is loved.

The Happiness of the Altruist of Faith: Level Four

It may be obvious at this point that the happiness of the altruist has many advantages over the happiness of the hedonist or the egoist. If happiness is to be found in meaningful activity and good relationships, altruists will have much more satisfying and happier lives than hedonists or egoists. In comparison with lower levels of happiness, level three happiness lasts longer, is more meaningful, and is more conducive to great friendships and positive relationships.

Yet something is still missing in level three. No one wants to be foolish and ignorant, yet we often find that we know only half-truths. Similarly, we want goodness,

[8] J. M. Gottman, J. Coan, S. Carrere, and C. Swanson, "Predicting Marital Happiness and Stability from Newlywed Interactions", *Journal of Marriage and the Family* 60 (1998): 5–22.

but every earthly good we choose is imperfect, limited, and in some way, however small, flawed. We want love, but even the most noble and beautiful of human loves cannot be perfect, because the two people who love each other are both imperfect. We want perfect truth, we want perfect goodness, and we want perfect love, but no mere human being can fulfill these transcendent desires. Only God, who embodies perfect truth, goodness, and love, can fulfill these transcendent desires of the human heart. So just as a kind of happiness (level three) is found in love and friendship with human beings, so too a kind of happiness is found in love and friendship with God (level four).

Of course, you may or may not believe in God. If you do believe in God, then this section of the book (and the other sections of the book that treat level four) will help you have a deeper understanding and appreciation of your faith. In discussing level four, I will focus in particular on Christian belief as articulated in Catholic tradition, but many of the same points will hold true for Orthodox Christian, Protestant, Jewish, and Muslim belief as well.

If you do not believe in God, these sections will be an opportunity for you to enhance your level three happiness by coming to a deeper understanding of many of your neighbors, colleagues, and fellow citizens. Since we cannot love what we do not in some way know, love and knowledge go together. By enhancing your knowledge of what another person believes, it is a chance to deepen love for that person, even if you do not share his beliefs.

It seems that everyone, whether or not he believes in God, *experiences* the imperfection of even the very best of earthly things: human pleasures, human achievements, and even human love. We can have the very best things in life in terms of level one, level two, and level three and yet still remain ultimately unsatisfied. C. S. Lewis developed this sense of longing into an argument for the existence of God: "Creatures are not born with desires unless satisfaction for these desires exists. A baby feels hunger; well, there is such a thing as food. A duckling wants to swim; well, there is such a thing as water. Men feel sexual desire; well, there is such a thing as sex. If I find in myself a desire which no experience in this world can satisfy, the most probable explanation is that I was made for another world."[9] Desires that we are born with, natural desires, are desires that can be satisfied.

People of faith believe that the human heart is made with a longing for Perfect Truth, Perfect Goodness, and Perfect Love. We were made to love God and to be loved by God. Level four happiness has to do with loving, praising, and thanking God and in turn experiencing God's love for us.

The higher levels of happiness—love of neighbor and love of God—go together. From a level three perspective, all human beings have innate dignity. From a level four perspective, human dignity is enhanced because each person is made in God's image and likeness, and each person is invited to have friendship with God. We are invited to focus on what is good in the other person, the gifts, talents, and potential that he has in virtue of being created and sustained by God. In encountering other people, the believer can look for the traces of God's action in the life of each

[9]C. S. Lewis, *Mere Christianity* (New York: HarperOne, 2001), 136.

person: "Whatever is true, whatever is honorable, whatever is just, whatever is pure, whatever is lovely, whatever is gracious, if there is any excellence, if there is anything worthy of praise, think about these things" (Phil 4:8).

For the Christian, love of neighbor is an obligation, an obligation that when fulfilled leads to deeper happiness. The two great commandments given by Jesus make this clear: "You shall love the Lord your God with all your heart, and with all your soul, and with all your mind.... You shall love your neighbor as yourself" (Mt 22:37, 39). If we truly love God, we will also love people, for they are made in his image and likeness. We cannot truly love God without also loving our neighbor. In the words of Dorothy Day, "I really only love God as much as I love the person I love the least." Indeed, the teachings of Jesus point us toward higher levels of happiness by guiding us toward this love: "A new commandment I give to you, that you love one another; even as I have loved you, that you also love one another" (Jn 13:34). As portrayed in the Gospels, the love of Jesus is universal, extending even to those who are generally hated and ostracized in society—the tax collector, the leper, the adulterer, and the thief. Christians are called to love in a similar way—universally, unconditionally, and sacrificially. This love is always dynamic because it responds to changes in the beloved as well as changes in the relationship.

We all want to be happier, and we all can be. We do not have to wait for that big promotion or for that party on Saturday night. Helping us achieve our true happiness—both here and eternally—is within our reach now with God's help. The more level three and level four activities that we choose, the happier we can be, even if our exterior circumstances do not change. A happier life can begin today with choosing philanthropic activities and growing in love of neighbor and of God.

That only God, and no human being, can fill our deepest longings is evident from experience. My wife Jennifer notes:

> The thing about hero-worshipping is that it rarely ends well. My first hero was Miss Lolly, my kindergarten teacher, upon whom I bestowed the title of "hero" before we had even met. During the summer before kindergarten, I decided that Miss Lolly and I would be best friends—simply because I was me and she was she. I told my mother, as we walked to school, that I was going to be Miss Lolly's favorite. With a bemused smile and a shrug of her shoulders, my mother said, "There are twenty-four students in your class, dear. You may have some competition."
>
> Sadly, not only was my mother correct about the competition (Jennifer Anderson already knew how to read!), but three weeks into the school year, when I had yet to be chosen as a line leader, it was discovered that Miss Lolly had completely overlooked me. Though she knew me by sight, my name, it seemed, was nowhere on her ledger. "That's odd", she mused to my mother. "What the heck?" I wondered to myself.
>
> Seven years later, upon receiving a form letter in response to a love letter written to Sean Cassidy, I swore off hero-worshipping altogether. To be honest, it was not that hard. My heroes, if I had pursued them, were Shelley Bruce, the lead in Broadway's *Annie*, and

Alan Alda. Thankfully, I had enough self-awareness to realize that neither actor was interested in striking up a friendship with a seventh-grade, B+ student from Seattle, Washington. And so I kept my heroes and our relationships where they belonged, in my fantasy life.

Until last Tuesday, when I got burned again. For years now, my literary hero has been David Sedaris, an American humor writer. His work is both out-rageously funny and, I think, deeply compassionate. Judging by the number of people willing to pay fifty dollars or more to hear Sedaris read his material, it is clear that I am not alone in my assessment. To say that I loved David Sedaris would be accurate. I considered him a writing mentor and believed that I read in his books (and by extension, his soul) a mutual love for humanity.

And so, when I discovered that he was coming to LA, I bought tickets. "This is my Mother's Day gift", I told my husband. "I can't wait." When Chris sug-gested I bring a book to be signed by Sedaris, I initially balked at the idea. "I don't know", I stammered. "I wouldn't know what to say." But in the intervening weeks, I decided that if Sedaris was signing books, I would bring mine. "All I want to say to him is that I admire his work and am drawn to his unique talent for exposing human weaknesses in a silly and yet com-passionate way", I told Chris.

Before I go on, I want you to reread part of that last sentence, beginning with "I admire", and then time yourself while you read it again. I can say it in four sec-onds. An appropriate response from Sedaris, something along the lines of, "Why, thank you. What a nice compliment. I hope you enjoy the show", should take, allowing for two inhalations, no more than another three or four seconds. Eye contact, considered by most to be a sign of respect and refinement, adds no additional time. Signing the book, assuming Sedaris has his own signature down to a science, should round the total tête-à-tête out to about ten seconds. In short, I was hoping for ten seconds of my hero's time.

What I got was much less—not in terms of seconds but in terms of quality. "What name?" Sedaris asked as I pressed the book forward. "Jennifer", I said, shocked that it took me a second to recall my own name. "With two *n*'s?" he asked. "Um ... yeah", I stammered. And then, as I opened my mouth to deliver my compliment, Sedaris inexplicably asked me what animal I wanted. "Animal?" I repeated, as though I had never heard the word. Looking up (and irritated), Sedaris repeated his question. "What animal would you like me to draw in your book?" It was clear that if he had to repeat his question, I would be risking both the signature and the animal, so I blurted out, "A cat." And then, before the anger washed over me, I offered my compliment awkwardly, and he accepted it—without eye contact, of course, because he was busy defacing my book with a cartoon cat.

David Sedaris may be a famous writer, but he can't doodle worth doody, and if he manages a kind of delicate balance between laughing at himself and laughing at others in his writing, he lacks such subtlety in person. I'm not sure what he estimates the average IQ of his readers to be, but if he thinks I can't tell when I'm being kept at arm's length via a doodle, he's off by ten or twenty points.

But as irritated as I was with Sedaris, I was more irritated with myself. Hero-worshipping? At my age? I suspected I would feel hollow, exposed, and stupid after meeting him. The first commandment was a clue, as was my common sense. I knew, before our brief exchange, that it's a rare hero who can meet a worshipper and make him feel infinitely valued.

In fact, we have a name for this rare hero—God. David Sedaris might be a great writer. He might even be a great person when he's not signing books. But I'm going back to God. The only one in that relationship hesitant to make eye contact is me.[10]

Hero-worship cannot make us happy, but can our spouse make us happy? From human experience and wisdom, it seems evident that marriage does not necessarily make a person happy, nor can a spouse make us happy. If someone tries to find happiness merely by level one activities, regardless of the marital status of the person, happiness will be elusive. Likewise, the egoist, married or not, will not find deep happiness. A spouse could give us level one or level two happiness (in terms of power or wealth), but no spouse can give us level three or level four happiness (though a spouse might facilitate or hamper such happiness).

[10] Modified slightly from Jennifer Kaczor, "You Shall Have No Strange Cats Before Me", Catholic Exchange, May 17, 2010, http://catholicexchange.com/you-shall-have-no-strange-cats-before-me/.

Yet, although marriage does not guarantee happiness, it does provide a concrete and realistic path to happiness. If someone says, "I'm going to get into shape this year" and leaves it at that, it is unlikely that the person will get in shape. By contrast, if someone says, "I'm going to walk for fifty minutes each day at 8:30 A.M.", that is more likely to happen. The resolution is concrete, specific, and actionable. In like manner, the married person does not say simply, "I'll love and serve somebody sometime." The married person has a very concrete and specific person to love. Spouses vow to love one another "in sickness and in health, for richer or poorer, in good times and in bad". What exactly is this love that spouses promise? It turns out that the answer to this question is more complicated and interesting than I had ever imagined.

The First Big Myth

"Love Is Simple"

The Reality: Both friendship and love are multidimensional realities often misunderstood at our peril.

In a shallow sense, everyone already knows what love is. We hear people say, "I love my best friend", "I love my fiancé", and "I love my daughter." Yet love for a best friend, love for a fiancé, and love for a daughter are obviously not in all respects the same. So love is a multifaceted concept.[1]

Still, every kind of love is alike in three elements: willing what is good for the beloved, an appreciation for the beloved, and a desire for unity with the beloved.[2] The form that these three elements takes, however, varies according to the kind of love involved.

As Alexander Pruss points out in his outstanding book *One Body: An Essay in Christian Sexual Ethics*, different forms of love involve a recognition of the *reality* of the beloved and the *relationship* of the lover and the beloved.

---

[1] See C. S. Lewis, *The Four Loves*, 2nd ed. (New York: Mariner Books, 1971).

[2] Alexander Pruss, *One Body: An Essay in Christian Sexual Ethics* (Notre Dame, Ind.: University of Notre Dame Press, 2012), 23.

He notes, for example, that if I love my daughter as if she were God, then I am not really loving my daughter, because my daughter is a human person, not God. If I love my daughter-as-God, I love a nonexistent being, an illusion. I must also love my daughter not simply as a young woman but as my daughter, taking into account the reality of our relationship as father and daughter.

Forms of love (spousal love, friendship love, parental love) differ from one another in three ways: (1) the goods that are appropriately willed for the beloved, (2) the kinds of appreciation that are fitting, and (3) the sorts of unity that are suitable for the relationship. Inappropriate loves involve a failure to take into account either the reality of the beloved or the relationship that one has to the beloved, or both the reality and the relationship.

Love responds to the reality of the beloved and to the distinctiveness of the relationship, and for this reason different forms of love arise. This chapter focuses on two vitally important forms of love, *philia* and *eros*, friendly love and erotic love. The first part of the chapter focuses on friendship; the second part of the chapter focuses on erotic love. A good marriage enjoys both kinds of love. In an ideal situation, husband and wife are erotic lovers as well as best friends.

Friendship and Marital Friendship

Researchers on marriage report that the best basis for a long-lasting and happy marriage is a solid friendship.[3] In

[3] Scott M. Stanley, Susan L. Blumberg, and Howard J. Markman, *Fighting for Your Marriage* (San Francisco: Jossey-Bass, 2001).

exploring friendship and marriage, we will now consider three different questions. First, what exactly is friendship? Second, what are the different kinds of friendship, and how do they differ from one another? Finally, what are the kinds of marital friendship?

What is friendship?

Aristotle's *Nicomachean Ethics* offers perhaps the most famous and influential consideration of the question, what is friendship? Aristotle suggests that friendship must involve mutual goodwill, shared activity, and time spent together. Each aspect of friendship is necessary for two people to be real friends rather than merely acquaintances, companions, or fellow travelers.

First, for a friendship to exist, we must have goodwill for the friend. We must desire good things for our friend for our friend's sake. Reciprocation is also needed. We cannot be friends with people if they do not have goodwill for us. Friendship is always a two-way street. Indeed, people often say things like, "I thought he was my friend until he stabbed me in the back."

But friendship involves more than just mutual goodwill. According to Aristotle, true friendship involves shared activity of some kind, whether it be mountain biking, analyzing fashion trends, or watching Monday Night Football. In order to become friends, not only must two people share activity together, but they must also share an emotional life. If tragedy strikes you, and you turn to someone you think is a friend only to find the person indifferent to your suffering, this person is not a true friend. Conversely, if you achieve a great triumph and in your joy share the good news with someone, and this person does not share your joy, again the person is not a friend.

What are the different kinds of friendship?

Let us turn now to the second question: What are the kinds of friendship, and how do they differ from one another? Love involves appreciation of the one loved. Since there are different kinds of things that one might appreciate about a friend, these different kinds of lovable characteristics distinguish different kinds of friendship. Aristotle notes that there seem to be three things that human beings find lovable: the useful, the pleasurable, and the excellent. From this, Aristotle concludes that there must be three kinds of friendship—a friendship of pleasure, a friendship of utility, and a friendship of excellence (sometimes translated as "friendship of virtue"). Saint Thomas Aquinas talks about another kind of excellence, infused virtue, given by God. So we can add a fourth kind of friendship, a friendship of infused virtue. Each one of these kinds of friendship is a possibility for us, and it is therefore important to recognize the qualities of each one.

Hedonists have friendships of pleasure. Friendships of pleasure, says Aristotle, are also common among the young. Here we might number "drinking buddies" in whose company we share the good times but not the bad. All friends enjoy jokes, reverie, and fun times together, but friendship of pleasure is limited only to such things.

However, what we take pleasure in is not usually the most lasting. The happiness of bodily pleasure arises quickly and leaves quickly. For example, it is fun to watch a TV show once; to watch the same episode back-to-back is tiresome. Seldom do the "party people" keep their lifestyle going much past college, and when they do, it is often pathetic. What we take pleasure in varies over the course of our lives. Pleasures are inconstant, so a friendship of pleasure will be unstable. That which delights the ten-year-old differs dramatically from that which delights the twenty-year-old, and that differs again from the pleasures characteristically enjoyed by the forty-year-old. I used to love to jump my BMX bike off ramps; I later loved to party; I now enjoy tickling my children. Like level one happiness, level one friendships are not long lasting. The friendships of the hedonist tend to be shallow, fleeting, and transitory. All friends have fun and enjoy each other's company, but a friendship of pleasure is based on fun alone.

While the hedonist has level one friendships of pleasure, the egoist has level two friendships of utility. I recall vividly my first experience with friends of utility. I was one of the oldest sophomores in my high school and so was able to drive before almost all of my classmates. Boy, was I popular! Classmates called weekend after weekend with great ideas about how we could pass the time. All they needed was a ride from me. Then, strangely, the next year the phone no longer rang. Now that my classmates had turned sixteen themselves, Kaczor and his Kitcar had become dispensable. A friend of utility is a person who has love for another not so much for who the person is but rather for what that person does for him. Insofar as what is useful changes frequently, friendships of utility last only so long as one party is useful to the other—for buying beer, for helping with homework, for rides around town. These friends are also more prone to disagreements because they basically have a business arrangement, an unspoken but assumed contract. Each fears giving too much and receiving too little.

The third kind of friendship described by Aristotle is a friendship of excellence, a level three friendship, or the friendship of the altruist. The Greek term *arete* is often translated as "virtue", but the word "virtue" can be a bit misleading to some contemporary readers. *Arete*, for Aristotle, meant an excellence, whether it be an excellent person, an excellent horse, or an excellent sword. Friends of excellence are certainly useful to us, and they also are pleasurable to be around, but they are loved not for what they give us or even for how they make us feel but because they are a certain kind of person, a truly good person.

When we speak of a "good person", we do not mean that the person is good at basketball, piano, or any particular endeavor. A good person—or better yet, an excellent person—is the person who enjoys level three and level four happiness to the full. The excellent person has characteristics, habits of the heart, that facilitate achieving level three and level four happiness. What characteristics make a person excellent?

Aristotle numbers courage, temperance, prudence, and justice as among the most important personal characteristics needed for happiness. These character traits enable a person consistently to enjoy loving other people. Without these characteristics, it seems difficult if not impossible to really love someone and maintain a friendship with someone over time.

Courage is firmness in pursuing what serves true happiness despite difficulties. Friends stick up for one another even at personal expense. They are not afraid to endure difficulties for the well-being of others or to persevere in doing good in trying circumstances. Temperance, the enjoyment of bodily pleasures in accordance with reason, also seems to be required of true friends. For example, it would be difficult to maintain a friendship with someone who had severe problems with alcohol or drug abuse. The addict invariably cares much more about getting high than about being a real friend. Prudence, or practical wisdom, discerns what is right and the right way of attaining what is right. True friends have the wisdom to know what the other needs and how he needs it—whether that is talking about something at length, staying silent but listening intently, or taking a middle ground. Finally, true friendship requires the persons to exercise the virtue of justice, as giving to each what is due. Rather than lie and practice deceit, a friend of virtue is truthful and honest and acts with integrity. At the very least, friends must practice justice toward one another if they are to remain friends. I cannot be friends with a person who steals from me, attacks me, lies to me, or murders me. A perfectly unjust person would be perfectly unsuited for any friendship.[4]

Excellent people, altruists, act in ways that accord with the deeper levels of happiness. Because they frequently do good acts, they have good habits, and habits are long lasting. These stable dispositions make possible a self-mastery,

[4]For much more on these virtues, see Christopher Kaczor and Thomas Sherman, *Thomas Aquinas on the Cardinal Virtues* (Ave Maria, Fla.: Sapientia, 2009).

ease, and joy in doing what is good and right. The excellent person delights in and freely practices good works and finds it painful to do the opposite. In so doing, an excellent person reinforces good habits. Hence, Aristotle reasons that a friendship of virtue will tend to be longer lasting than a friendship of utility or pleasure. Although friends of virtue are also pleasant and helpful to one another, friends of virtue love each other for who they are, not simply for the pleasure or the help that they get from each other. Just as the happiness of level three and four outlasts that of level one and two, so too virtue or excellence of character seems to be longer lasting than either the useful or the pleasurable.

Finally, a fourth kind of friendship is friendship of infused virtue, or of infused excellence. A person gains acquired virtues through repeated level three and four choices, but a person gains infused virtues through a gift of God's grace working in the person's life. People with infused virtues have become excellent because of God's work in their lives. A level four friendship of infused virtue perfects all the good elements of a level three friendship. These friendships of infused virtue are strong not merely through the power of the individuals but through the power of God.

What are the different kinds of marital friendship?

We have distinguished four kinds of friendship: a friendship of pleasure, a friendship of utility, a friendship of excellence, and a friendship of infused virtue. These four kinds of friendship lead to four kinds of marital friendship:

a marital friendship of pleasure, a marital friendship of utility, a marital friendship of excellence, and a marital friendship of infused virtue.

For those with sexual passion between them, friendships
of pleasure involve sexual pleasure. Think "friends with
benefits". It is clearly possible to initiate a marriage on this
basis. The beauty of a woman or handsomeness of a man
and the delights of sex have led many a person down the
aisle.

But the question arises, would this be the best kind of
marital friendship? Ben Franklin suggests that a happy marriage must be based on more than an amorous fixation:

> Well, they are married, and have taken their full of
> love. The young spark's rant is over, he finds his imagi-
> nary Goddess mere flesh and blood with the addition of
> a vain, affected, silly girl; and when his theatrical dress
> is off, she finds he was a lying, hot brained coxcomb.
> Thus, come to their senses, and the mask thrown off,
> they look at one another like utter strangers, persons
> come out of a trance; he finds by experience that he
> fell in love with his own ideas and she with her own
> vanity. Thus plucked from the soaring heights of their
> warm and irregular passions, they are vexed at and
> ashamed at themselves first, and heartily hate each other
> afterwards.[5]

Even for the most sexually active, sexual activity perhaps accounts for a small fraction of one's total time with

[5] Ben Franklin, "Reflections on Courtship and Marriage", in *Wing to Wing,
Oar to Oar: Readings on Courting and Marrying*, ed. Leon Kass and Amy Kass
(Notre Dame, Ind.: University of Notre Dame Press, 2000), 409–10. The spell-
ing has been modernized.

a spouse. Choosing a spouse primarily because of sexual compatibility tends not to end well because of the inherent instability of a life devoted to bodily pleasure. The marital friendship of hedonists is exceedingly unlikely to celebrate a tenth, or even a fifth, wedding anniversary.

Some egoists have marital friendships of utility. A marital friendship of utility is a kind of business in which each spouse negotiates for the best allotment of resources and the lightest burden to bear. Marriage is a fifty-fifty deal. Years ago, I met a couple who took this principle quite literally. She cooked on Monday, Wednesday, and Friday; he cooked on Tuesday, Thursday, and Saturday. They alternated cooking on Sunday. They split the laundry, and everything else, with mathematical precision. She did not know where his sock drawer was; and from the looks of it, he did not either. I did not ask how they handled nursing their baby for fear of robbing the baby of breast milk. I thought it odd that such an arrangement was necessary. My college roommate, Chad, and I in college had not sworn eternal love for one another, and yet he often threw in my towels with his laundry.

It is not hard to find examples of marital friendships of utility. Think of the twenty-six-year-old model Anna Nicole Smith and her eighty-nine-year-old billionaire husband, Texas oilman J. Howard Marshall. She gets $450 million after his death; he gets a "trophy wife". Less blatant cases happen frequently despite the truth of the maxim that whoever marries for money earns every penny of it. However, a marital friendship of utility need not be as crass as mere economics. Consider the thirty-something woman with a ticking biological clock, and the late-thirty-something man whose bachelor days are becoming a bit of an embarrassment to his business. People in these situations sometimes marry someone whom they neither love nor respect simply to meet certain needs. If Aristotle is correct about the duration of friendships of utility, then we can expect these marriages of utility frequently to end in divorce.

It is also possible to have a marital friendship of excellence and a marital friendship of infused virtue. Thomas Aquinas taught that marriage could be the greatest kind of friendship: "The greater a friendship is, the more solid and long lasting will it be. *Now there seems to be the greatest friendship between husband and wife*, for they are united not only in the act of fleshly union, which produces a certain gentle association even among beasts, but also in the partnership of the whole range of domestic activity."[6] Just as there can be marital friendships of utility or pleasure, so too there can be marital friendships of excellence and infused excellence. To have this kind of friendship, both husband and wife must be virtuous people. So identity as a hedonist, an egoist, or an altruist is relevant not just to finding happiness but also to enjoying a lasting and satisfying marital friendship.

Erotic Love

Most marriages, at least today, involve not simply some kind of friendship but also erotic love. Good marriages last

---

[6] Thomas Aquinas, *Summa contra Gentiles*, trans. Vernon J. Bourke (Notre Dame, Ind.: University of Notre Dame Press, 1975), III, ch. 123, n. 6, p. 148, (emphasis mine).

because of the friendship between the spouses, but most marriages begin because of erotic love. Despite the common experience of falling in love, the nature of erotic love remains quite elusive, even after centuries of reflection.

Especially for the young, there can be important questions about whether or not a person really is in love with someone else. For the parents of the young, erotic love can also cause no little anxiety. It would seem that both parents and young people have a vested interest in figuring out what "love" (that is, erotic love) really is.

The nature of erotic love

Perhaps the most famous discussion of erotic love is found in Plato's *Symposium*, a dialogue in which friends and lovers who are freely sharing wine together give speeches in praise of love. The comic playwright Aristophanes delivers the most memorable oration of the night, a speech about the genesis of eros.

Originally, Aristophanes says, primordial human beings were circular in shape, roughly resembling cylindrically shaped conjoined twins.[7] These primordial human beings, joined at the back, had four arms, four legs, and two faces. Their round shape enabled them to travel with great speed by rolling around in a manner akin to acrobats or gymnasts cartwheeling. Although their appearance may seem bizarre to us, they were powerful creatures whose pride led them to rebel against the gods. As punishment, in

[7] Plato, *Symposium*, trans. Michael Joyce, in *The Collected Dialogues of Plato*, ed. Edith Hamilton and Huntington Cairns (Princeton: Princeton University Press, 1961), 527–74 at 545.

order to weaken and disorder the creatures and thereby make them less of a threat and more useful to the gods, Zeus split them in two.

As a result, erotic desire arose as each creature yearned to find its lost half. Eros in all its forms is a desire for unity—to find our "soul mate", the one who completes us. According to Aristophanes, the longing for union is given a specific outlet for consummation in this new arrangement, sexual intercourse. The craving to be united leads erotic lovers ardently to desire to be together, within each other's sight, and to enjoy sexual intercourse with one another.

It is instructive to compare the Platonic account of creation given by Aristophanes with the biblical account of creation found in Genesis. Although both depict erotic love as a yearning for unity, Aristophanes' account of eros differs significantly from the account of Adam and Eve in Genesis. In Genesis, eros is part of the original blessing of creation. God enjoins Adam and Eve to be fruitful and multiply prior to the fall. For Aristophanes, by contrast, eros arose as a result of a divine punishment for wrongdoing. Before rebellion, and before punishment by the gods, there was no eros and indeed no procreation. Yet in both Aristophanes and in Genesis, the first human beings long for unity.

As demonstrated by the tale of Aristophanes, the first mistake people make about erotic love is to elevate eros so that it becomes divine. Phaedrus, another speaker in the *Symposium*, holds that love is not only a god but the most primordial of the gods. In this view, the deeply human character of erotic love becomes obscured, and it turns out that we are not so much in love with the beloved as an individual human person. Rather, we love the divine transcendent in which the beloved somehow participates. In this view, love and sex become utterly serious, the closest link to the divine possible. Love and sex may be viewed as a sort of savior that, when enjoyed, satisfies the deepest longing of the human heart and leads to perfect human fulfillment.[8]

The second mistake people make about erotic love is to reduce it to animal instincts, physical processes, and biological chemistry. Eryximachus, another speaker in the *Symposium*, holds that love is found not just among humans but also among animals and plants. Sigmund Freud's reduction of love to lust is another example. In this view, the human experience of being in love is nothing more than a mistaken apprehension of physical, animal desire with no more real significance than any other desire shared with animals—such as being hungry. The distinctly human character of erotic love again disappears from view.

Martha Nussbaum corrects the first type of error, treating love and eros with a divine solemnity, by highlighting the comedic aspect of eros.

> As we hear Aristophanes' distant myth of this passionate groping and grasping, we are invited to think how odd, after all, it is that bodies should have these holes and projections in them, odd that the insertion of a projection into an opening should be thought, by ambitious and intelligent beings, a matter of the deepest concern. ... From the outside we cannot help laughing. They want to be gods—and here they are,

---

[8] See William F. May's treatment of sex as divine in his article "Four Mischievous Theories of Sex", in Kass and Kass, *Wing to Wing*, 189–201.

running around anxiously trying to thrust a piece of
themselves inside a hole; or perhaps more comical still,
waiting in the hope that some hole of theirs will have
something thrust into it.[9]

It *is* funny to rethink sexuality and eros in these terms.
The comedian Aristophanes plies his trade in depicting a
side of eros that thus far had been underappreciated by the
earlier speeches in the *Symposium*. The seriousness with
which we take eros and its distinctive act, the thrusting of
a piece of ourselves into a hole or the receiving of a piece
of another into ourselves, would be utterly ridiculous
were we to substitute for the coupling of sexual organs
putting our ear lobe into another's outer ear canal. It is
hard to imagine intense jealousy, devastating betrayals, or
soaring feelings of unity resulting from the intercourse of
ear lobe and ear canal. Indeed, the unity of ears utterly
lacks even the intimacy and excitement of kissing. Great
drama can hinge on unity between some human organs,
but not all.

However, this indicates that in love and sex, something else is going on besides simply the unity of holes and
projections. Eros certainly can be funny, but to see only
comedy and nothing else is also a failure to capture much
of human experience. Comedy alone does not properly
describe the power and drive of eros. In emphasizing
the primordial drive of eros, it might be concluded that
eros is nothing other than the primordial urge of animal
attraction.

[9] Martha Nussbaum, *The Fragility of Goodness: Luck and Ethics in Greek Tragedy and Philosophy* (New York: Cambridge University Press, 1986), 172–73.

The differences between erotic love and mere sexual attraction

The characterization of eros as merely sexual attraction is perhaps more common today than thinking eros to be a kind of god. However, erotic love, or being "in love", cannot be reduced to a mere kind of animal magnetism, a physical attraction.

Yet it is easy to confuse eros and physical attraction because the two have much in common. Both are intense, passionate, and deeply sexual. Both can intoxicate, addict, and spur to valiant action. Both can begin with a glance and can be entirely spent in nine and a half weeks. Each aspect of this commonality merits its own attention.

Eros and sexual attraction share intensity. By intensity, I mean that both eros and sexual attraction can fully grip our attention. We are drawn, as if by a tractor beam, to the beautiful person. When an extremely attractive person or our beloved enters the room, everyone else disappears from view. This passion is the polar opposite of a casual indifference and is linked in important ways to sexuality. Eros and sexual attraction are for the beautiful, and we desire to possess, enjoy, and have intercourse with the beautiful.

Eros and physical attraction can intoxicate the mind, warping a normal sense of time and judgment. To be with the beautiful or the beloved is the goal, the achievement of which can seem worth virtually any price. And, as anyone who has asked a person of doubtful reply for a date will tell, to find beauty and eros are worth the risk of humiliation. Love dares all, and so sometimes does powerful sexual attraction.

Eros and physical attraction can also both share immediacy. One knows generally immediately, and almost always after a few minutes of conversation, whether one finds another person sexually attractive. Eros can be similarly immediate. Although some couples fall in love over time, it is also true that we speak of "love at first sight". How often have we heard people say that they knew right away that their beloved was "the one"?

But the alacrity of the genesis of eros and physical attraction is sometimes matched by the brevity of their duration. We can fall in love in a flash, but we can also fall out of love before we know it. Physical beauty alone, even among the most beautiful, hardly ensures a long-lasting or satisfying relationship, as the host of super beautiful, short-lived celebrity couples makes clear.

Although eros and physical attraction have much in common, it is important not to overlook the differences between mere sexual magnetism and erotic love. Erotic love yearns for expression in sexual acts; mere attraction is exhausted in sexual acts. Erotic love focuses on one particular beautiful person; mere attraction is for any number of beautiful people. Erotic love is a preoccupation with the whole person of the beloved—the way he laughs, writes letters, and cares for friends. Mere sexual attraction focuses on a reduced conception of the person as an actual or potential sexual partner. This kind of desire is akin to other animal desires, such as hunger for food. It is precisely here that we can find the difference between mere sexual desire and love: we hunger for any kind of food, but erotic love is only for one particular person. If I want nachos, any given plate of nachos will do. If I love Jennifer Turner Kaczor, only Jennifer Turner Kaczor will do. Mere sexual desire seeks any given attractive partner; erotic love seeks the beloved and the beloved alone.

A final way to consider the difference between erotic love and mere sexual attraction is in terms of the desired duration of relationship. Although both sexual attraction and erotic love are notoriously short-lived in duration, erotic love wishes to be with the beloved forever. Mere sexual attraction, on the other hand, wants its object of affection right now. Eros seeks eternity; mere sexual attraction seeks rapidity.

Alexander Pruss points out that romantic love (a form of eros) is truly a form of love: "In romantic love, the other's good as a sexual being is willed in a way that involves the lover's sexuality, the other is appreciated as a sexual being in and through the lover's sexual desires, and the lover strives for, or at least is drawn to, a sexual union with the beloved, a union that consummates the love."[10] Seeking the good of the other and being drawn to unity distinguishes romantic love from mere sexual attraction.

The ultimate goal of erotic love

Aristophanes notes that the couple touched by eros wishes for nothing less than complete unity—to be together forever, to be forged into one. Near the conclusion of his speech, Aristophanes says:

> Now, supposing Hephaestus [the blacksmith god] were to come and stand over [the lovers] with his tool bag as they lay there side by side, and suppose he were to ask, Tell me, my dear creatures, what do you really want with one another. And suppose they didn't know

[10] Pruss, *One Body*, 87.

what to say, and he went on, How would you like to
be rolled into one, so that you could always be together
day and night, and never be parted again? Because if
that's what you want, I can easily weld you together,
and then you can live your two lives in one, and, when
the time comes, you can die a common death and still
be two-in-one in the lower world. Now, what do
you say? Is that what you'd like me to do? And would
you be happy if I did? We may be sure, gentlemen,
that no lover on earth would dream of refusing such
an offer, for not one of them could imagine a happier
fate. Indeed, they would be convinced that this was just
what they'd been waiting for—to be merged, that is,
into an utter oneness with the beloved.[11]

According to Aristophanes, eros is most fundamentally the
desire for a comprehensive unity with the beloved. For this
reason, those under the spell of eros desire sexual relations,
for in the sexual act bodies become intimately joined, and
during sexual climax even the psychic distinction between
lover and beloved becomes blurred. The desire for a comprehensive union is at the core of eros, not merely a desire
for sexual relations. Mere sexual relations with the beloved
alone would not satisfy the person deeply in love.

Indeed, erotic love's general drive for unity can also be
expressed in many nonsexual ways, such as sharing meals
together, laughing, and living together. One way of real-
izing the dream of eros is to enter into a comprehensive
union with another, a union that goes by the name of
marriage. It is to this subject that we now turn.

<hr />

[11] Plato, *Symposium*, 192d–e, 545n12.

The Second Big Myth

"Marriage Is a Fifty-Fifty Contract"

The Reality: Marriage is a 100 *percent—*100 *percent covenant.*

I am not a priest, a politician, a soldier, or a judge. I have taken only one oath or vow in my life: "I, Christopher, take you, Jennifer, to be my wife. I promise to be true to you in good times and in bad, in sickness and in health, until death do us part. I will love you and honor you all the days of my life."

Before the vow, we were engaged. After the vow, we were married. If someone balks at taking the vows, even if he has walked down the aisle, that person is not yet married. Vows, oaths, and promises are what philosophers call "performative utterances". Saying the words changes the reality. After promising, there becomes an obligation to do what is promised. Before promising, there was no such obligation. In a similar way, when people take an oath of office, they take on new responsibilities and change their identity. The judicial nominee becomes the judge, the potential soldier becomes the private first class, the president-elect becomes the president.

So when the couple exchanges the marriage vows, they also take on a new identity. Through their mutual consent, they become husband and wife. Now, most people are not elected president, senator, or governor and so do not take oaths of office. But the marriage vow is the one oath that the great majority of people take in the course of their lives. To take a vow is to commit oneself in the most serious, profound, and human way. No animal takes an oath—but a human being can make such solemn commitments.

What commitment did I make? What exactly is promised in the marital vow? In particular, what is meant by "love" in this vow?

The Promise of a Lifetime: Love and Marriage

People rightly associate marriage with erotic love. So perhaps in the vow, each person promises to love the other with eros. As noted in the previous chapter, eros is the desire for a comprehensive unity with another. Alexander Pruss puts the point as follows: "Given that romantic love calls for the deepest possible union at all levels of the person, especially including the physical level, it is plausible that romantic love calls for something like this kind of commitment, namely, for a marriage 'until death do us part' ".[1] When you are in love, you want to be united with the beloved in body, mind, and spirit. You desire to be united with the beloved not just now but in the future. So perhaps the new married couple have promised always to

[1] Alexander Pruss, *One Body: An Essay in Christian Sexual Ethics* (Notre Dame, Ind.: University of Notre Dame Press, 2013), 162.

have erotic love for each other regardless of circumstances such as health and wealth.

However, this understanding of the marriage vows as promising erotic love faces a difficulty. Vows and oaths are kinds of promises, and meaningful promises are always about things that are in the control of the person making the promise. For instance, I cannot control the weather, so it does not make sense for me to make a promise to you about the weather. I cannot promise that on May 15 of each year, precisely two inches of snow will fall in Los Angeles.

So the marriage vow could be about only erotic love if erotic love is something that we can control. But it is obvious that we cannot directly control erotic love. This is why people speak of "*falling* in love", since falling is not something that we control but something that happens to us. It would be absurd for someone to command you, "Fall in love with the next person you see"; likewise, if you are already in love, it would be absurd for someone to command you, "Just choose not to be in love anymore." Since erotic love is not subject to choice, it is not something about which we can promise.

If the love of eros is not promised in the marriage vow, then perhaps the love of philia or friendship is what is promised. Perhaps the couple are vowing solemnly to be friends—whether friends of virtue, utility, or pleasure—so long as they both shall live. Unlike erotic love, friendship is not something that just happens to you, because friendship always involves choice.

However, friendship, as mentioned earlier, also involves not just the choice of one person but the choice of two people to have mutual goodwill. And of course, mutual goodwill is not something that one person can do unilaterally. In the marriage vow, each person agrees to love the other. This decision to love is something that can indeed be controlled by each person individually. We can choose to love someone else even if he does not choose to love us back. We cannot make someone else love us, so we cannot ever promise "mutual goodwill" insofar as this presupposes the free choice of someone else. So the marriage vow is not the promise to love a person with philia, since, like erotic love, philia is not something that an individual has the power to control. Good marriages are built and last because of deep friendship, but friendship is not what is promised.

So the promise of the marriage vow is not the commitment always to feel the pull of erotic love. We cannot directly control our emotions, longings, and desires. Nor is the oath of marriage the promise always to be friends, since we cannot control anyone but ourselves, and friendship necessarily involves mutual goodwill. So what is promised? In marriage, the spouse promises to love not with eros or philia but with marital *agape*.

What is agape? Perhaps the most famous description of agape is given by Saint Paul:

> Love [*agape*] is patient and kind; love is not jealous or boastful; it is not arrogant or rude. Love does not insist on its own way; it is not irritable or resentful; it does not rejoice at wrong, but rejoices in the right. Love bears all things, believes all things, hopes all things, endures all things. Love never ends. (1 Cor 13:4–8)

Agape is the kind of love that is a decision, not an emotion. You can be incredibly angry with someone and still have agape for that person. Feelings are transitory. Agape—in bearing all things, enduring all things, and never failing—is not. Feelings may or may not lead to action. Agape is ordered to action—beneficial action.

Agape involves three elements: (1) willing what is good for the one loved, (2) appreciating the good of the one loved, and (3) desiring a unity with the one loved.[2] Agape is found in many nonmarital relationships. Take the example of Blessed Mother Teresa's Missionaries of Charity. First, these sisters have goodwill for the poor and work to alleviate their suffering and hardship. Second, these good sisters are united with the poor both in the sisters' manner of life and in their desire to help the poor materially and spiritually. Third, the Missionaries of Charity appreciate the good that is found in the poor, namely, the way in which they reflect the hidden face of Christ.

Marital love specifies a particular form of agape with a real unity, appreciation, and determination of the will reflecting who the spouses are and their relationship to each other. Although the Missionaries of Charity and spouses both have agape, the love of the spouses is different because they are united, appreciate the good in the other, and have goodwill in a distinctive way. First, their goodwill for one another reflects their identity as spouses and their relationship as spouses. Second, they appreciate one another in a particular respect, as spouses and as sexual beings. Finally, the spouses are unified *as marital partners* to one another. Their unity is not simply in one activity or another; rather, their unity consists, in part, in taking

[2] Here I borrow and slightly adapt the definition offered by Pruss, *One Body*, 28.

on a new identity as long as they both shall live. The man becomes a *husband* to the woman, and the woman becomes a *wife* to the man. The two individuals become a "we", a married couple. They share in their unification as spouses, a unification that fittingly includes bodily unification in a sexual way. What kind of unity is a marital unity? To answer this question, we must distinguish covenant marriages from contract unions.

The Difference between a Covenant Marriage and a Contract Union

In American culture, many couples who get married go through ceremonies similar to the one that my wife and I chose. The groom wears a tuxedo; the bride wears a white dress. Their friends and family witness the ceremony in which vows are exchanged, and everyone celebrates at the reception. But even though outward appearances may be similar, the types of marriage formed may in fact be very different. My wife and I formed what you can call a covenant marriage, but many people form a contract union.

It is important to be clear on this matter. To get married is one of the most important choices a person can make, so it is vitally important to understand what it is that is promised in marriage. In order to be fair to a potential spouse and in order for a person to make an informed decision about marriage himself, a person must understand the content of the marriage vow. Both people should be explicit in terms of what they understand marriage to be (covenant versus contract), so as to make it fair to both people entering into marriage.

There are a number of important differences between a contract union and a covenant marriage. First, and most important, a covenant marriage involves unconditional love. A contract union involves only conditional love. Notice the unconditional nature of the traditional marriage vow: for better or for worse, in sickness and in health, until death do us part. There are no conditions for this spousal love. By contrast, a contract union involves conditional love for the husband or wife. Even if the couple exchange the traditional marriage vow, the husband or the wife actually holds back from the unconditional commitment promised in the vow. Rather than give themselves no matter what, their love is limited by certain unspoken demands that, if not met, will lead to termination of the relationship. They believe, even if they do not actually say, "I'll love you so long as you provide this or that. I'll love you so long as you do not do this or that." By contrast, a covenant marriage involves loving the person as your spouse with unconditional love. Death alone ends the covenant marriage, since at death the bodily human being who was the spouse no longer exists.

Most people like the idea of loving their spouse unconditionally and receiving unconditional love from their husband or wife. However, some people are sceptical that this kind of unconditional love is possible. Yet most people have had the good fortune of experiencing unconditional love, usually from their own mother or father (hopefully both). My parents would be devastated if I turned into a mass murderer, but they would love me even in this case. Indeed, at the trials of cold-blooded killers, one can often see the parents of the accused—devastated, afraid, and desperate—still loving and supporting their child. Unconditional love is also possible in other relationships—including marriage. In a covenant marriage, husband and wife promise to love each other unconditionally as husband or as wife.

This leads to the second difference between covenant marriage and contract union. Covenant marriages are indissoluble—the marital union remains until death. Therefore, someone who leaves a spouse and has sex with another person commits adultery. By contrast, contract unions are dissoluble. Either party is free to divorce the spouse and marry another person.

Now, some people like the idea of dissolubility. If the marriage becomes difficult, especially if it becomes extremely troubled, they can divorce their spouse and seek a better relationship. But dissolubility is necessarily linked with conditional love. If husband and wife love each other as spouses unconditionally, this leads to indissolubility. If a couple are free to divorce one another and marry somebody else, the couple necessarily have only conditional love for each other. Either a marriage has unconditional love and is therefore indissoluble, or the union is dissoluble and therefore based on only conditional love.

Third, a covenant marriage, again unlike a contract marriage, creates a family bond between the spouses. Family bonds are permanent ties that cannot be undone. Your mother is your mother whether she is a good mother or a bad mother. Similarly, if you have a brother or a sister, your sibling is your sibling whether you see him daily, rarely, or never, whether your sibling is your best friend or a big fiend. Once married, a person can no more choose not to be a husband or a wife to his spouse than your mother can choose not to be your mother or than you can choose not to be a son or a daughter. By contrast, in a contract union, no permanent family bond is created between the spouses; rather, a working relationship is created. When the marital relationship is not working, it may simply be terminated and another one created in its place.

Finally, in a covenant marriage, the spouses make a gift of themselves as spouses to each other. In the wedding vows, the husband gives himself to his wife. Part of each one of us is what we shall become in the future; therefore, when the man gives himself as a husband to his wife, he does so both now and as long as they both shall live. At the ceremony, he gives himself in terms of his verbal consent; later, when they are alone, he will give himself to her in an intimate bodily way. The bride returns the gift of self, giving herself to him as his wife both now and as long as they both shall live, both in word through the vows and in body through sexual intercourse. The verbal consent to marriage and the bodily consent to the marital act ratify the covenant of marriage. The spoken words manifest a gift of self, and the sexual act embodies a gift of self. In both words and in deeds, they hold nothing back but give themselves entirely as spouses to each other.

In a contract union, by contrast, the couple exchange not themselves but goods and services. They give something of themselves but also hold something of themselves back, whether in body or spirit or both. They might reserve for themselves the right to sever the relationship and start a new marriage with another person in the future, or to refuse to give themselves in a bodily way if physical attraction wanes, permanently denying the other spouse sexual intercourse. As Joshua Schultz points out, "To insist that marital vows become meaningless when two people have grown apart, for instance, is to suppose that a marriage exists only where an exchange of goods extrinsic to the marriage occurs to the satisfaction of each partner, and that the marriage vows are unjust (and so null and void) otherwise. But if the subject is [covenant] marriage itself, the economic vocabulary of exchange germane to contracts is inappropriate to marriage."[3] Covenant marriage involves an unconditional and unreserved gift of oneself as spouse. A contract union involves an exchange of goods and services only so long as both desire it. A contract union can be a fifty-fifty deal; covenant marriage is a 100 percent commitment from both parties.

It perhaps becomes clear why those in the thralls of erotic love desire covenant marriage. They want a comprehensive union with one another. They wish to be united as closely as possible with the beloved, not just now but forever, not just in words but also in body. A mere contractual union would not satisfy their desires.

Roger Scruton identifies another difference between a vow and a contractual promise.[4] A solemn vow like that of covenant marriage is never fulfilled in time; a contractual promise is. In agreeing to paint a house, the painter and the owner might agree, "This house shall be painted by August 11, or no further payment shall be made." There is a date of termination. A vow, by contrast, is for the whole of life. A contractual promise can be undone by

---

[3] Joshua Schulz, "Indissoluble Marriage: A Defense", *Logos* 15, no. 2 (2012): 124.

[4] Roger Scruton, "Sacrilege and Sacrament", in *The Meaning of Marriage: Family, State, Market, and Morals*, ed. Robert P. George and Jean Bethke Elshtain (New York: Scepter, 2010), 10–11.

mutual agreement of the parties involved. By contrast, a vow can only be dishonored but never revoked and canceled. With a contract, the cost-benefit analysis is known beforehand—the house owner gets a painted house, while the painter gets three thousand dollars. With a vow, the cost and benefit are unknown. It is a daring promise to make a vow, but those in love have the courage to do so.

That was the main reason why I was nervous on my wedding day. It was not simply the tuxedo, the ill-fitting shoes, my bride's beautiful white dress, and the fact that 350 of our friends and family were focusing their attention on us. It was the knowledge that I was taking my future into my hands and joining that future irrevocably with someone else's future. Consenting to a covenant marriage is something like becoming a father or a mother. Parents never know what the future holds when welcoming a child into the family. All that is certain is that they are parents for as long as that child shall live. They might be great parents or lousy parents, and the child may be a joy or a trial, but they remain parents. So too I did not know who Jennifer would become, and she did not know who I would become, five, ten, or twenty years later. The only certainty was that she would change and that I would change, and that whatever these changes were, we would remain husband and wife so long as we both should live.

Divorce for Irreconcilable Differences

What causes people to hesitate to enter a covenant marriage? Some people think that half of marriages lack unconditional love and end in divorce, and so they hesitate to commit themselves to covenant marriage. In fact, as marriage researchers David Popenoe and Barbara Dafoe Whitehead point out, "The divorce rate has been dropping since the early 1980s. If today's divorce rate continues unchanged into the future, the chances that a marriage contracted this year [2001] will end in divorce before one partner dies has been estimated to be between 40 and 45 percent."[5] As Michael Medved points out, "If this constitutes the first marriage for both of you, there's a better than 70% chance that you will remain married until one of you dies."[6] Attending college, even if not graduating, further reduces the likelihood of divorce. Weekly attendance at church services reduces the likelihood of divorce 20 percent for women and 40 percent for men.[7] The likelihood of divorce is not the flip of a coin; it is deeply influenced by our own activities and choices—most especially the decision to love our spouse unconditionally.

Some people cite irreconcilable differences as a reason for divorce. Irreconcilable differences include divergent

[5] David Popenoe and Barbara Dafoe Whitehead, "The Top Ten Myths of Divorce", The National Marriage Project Information Brief, April 2001, Mississippi State University, http://msucares.com/marriage/research/myths_of _divorce.pdf. See also Joshua R. Goldstein, "The Leveling of Divorce in the United States", *Demography* 36 (1999): 409–14; Arthur J. Norton and Louisa F. Miller, *Marriage, Divorce and Remarriage in the 1990s* (Washington, D.C.: U.S. Bureau of the Census, 1992).

[6] Michael Medved, "Al, Tipper and the Myth of a 'Good Divorce'", June 23, 2010, http://townhall.com/columnists/michaelmedved/2010/06/23/al, _tipper_and_the_myth_of_a_good_divorce/page/full.

[7] These statistics come from the 2006 General Social Survey data as interpreted by Brian Holler of George Mason University, "Religion = Romance? Divorce Rates vs. Church Attendance", *Thinking on the Margin* (blog), February 14, 2011, http://thinkingonthemargin.blogspot.com/2011/02/religion-romance-divorce-rates-vs.html.

views on how to spend money, how to divide labor, how often to have sex, how often to allow the in-laws to visit, how to celebrate holidays, how many kids to have, and how to discipline the kids. We need not mention politics, social habits, religious views, and lifestyle choices. If you enter a contract union and later find that you have married someone with whom you have irreconcilable differences, you simply divorce the person and destroy the union.

Let us say that I discover that Jennifer and I have irreconcilable differences. She wants to live in Boston, and I want to live in Kansas. She wants ten cats; I am happy with one. She wants to canonize Barack Obama; I am a fan of Rush Limbaugh. If I have a contract marriage, I simply divorce her and look for someone with whom I am more compatible.

Fortunately, I find her! My new wife Stephanie passionately loves living in Kansas, wants only one cat, and is addicted to conservative talk radio. Irreconcilable differences abolished! But after a while, I discover that Stephanie and I also have our own disagreements. She likes to shop; I will not spend a dime. She is nonreligious; I am Catholic. She stays up late; I go to bed early. So after years of fighting about these things, we divorce.

Okay, the next time I will get it right. I sign up for an online dating service, and I carefully limit my search to the desired characteristics: Kansas loving, Catholic, early riser, talk-radio listening, one-cat loving, frugal, and super beautiful, just for good measure. Finally, Beatrice enters my life. Things could not be more ideal and perfect for us. Yet after a while, I discover that even we have our own irreconcilable differences: we disagree over how frequently to invite guests to our house, how often to have sex, and how to celebrate holidays. Urgh. In fact, this scenario is not far-fetched. Many people believe that their second or third marriage will be successful. In reality, the rate of divorce for second marriages is much higher than that for first marriages, and the rate of divorce for third marriages is still higher.[8]

The point is simple. No matter how many spouses a person goes through, irreconcilable differences will always be present. All couples—happy couples, miserable couples, and divorced couples—have irreconcilable differences. These differences became evident at a formal dinner for faculty at Loyola Marymount University. My wife recounts:

Good news: my husband has been promoted. For the past twelve years he has worked not only diligently, but brilliantly, to achieve his promotion. And now, at the relatively young age of forty, he is a full professor. What this means for me, of course, is a free dinner.

As befits such an achievement, the president of LMU holds a formal dinner for all faculty members who have secured either tenure or a promotion. It is called, reasonably enough, "The Rank and Tenure Dinner", and awardees are encouraged to bring a guest. More often than not, this means a spouse. And so, on a warm June night, in the president's elegant dining room, we gathered—the erudite and the extras.

[8] Goldstein, "Leveling of Divorce"; Andrew Cherlin, *Marriage, Divorce, Remarriage* (Cambridge, Mass.: Harvard University Press, 1992).

Now, you may think I am being a bit hard on myself and my counterparts—referring to us as "the extras". Before the dinner, I would have agreed. "Really," I would have argued, "there is no discernible difference between those with PhDs and those without. We are equally intelligent." I might have insisted, "And certainly more practical. My husband has not only worn two different-colored socks to work, but he has worn two different shoes!" Having never done anything so silly, I would actually have concluded that I had the right to feel vastly superior.

How then to explain what happened last night? After much thought, I can only conclude that all of the jokes about professors exist for the same reason that blond jokes exist. Deep down, we, the extras (and quite possibly the brunettes), are jealous. In spite of their absentmindedness, professors are, by nature, thoughtful creatures, less likely to speak before thinking than the rest of us—less likely, in short, publicly to humiliate themselves.

"The Humiliations of the Extras" began last night, as humiliations often do, over dessert. My husband's colleague, a tall man in theology, asked me how I thought I would manage while my husband was away for twelve days this coming summer. "Won't you be exhausted," he asked chivalrously, "taking care of the children by yourself?" I could simply have said yes. He wanted me to say yes. He wanted to compliment me on my mothering skills, wanted to see me as the ideal wife—the platonic version of wife and mother: loving and sacrificial, fragile yet competent. But because I am not a professor, and do not habitually think before I speak (and because I was distracted by an excellent peach melba), I told the tall man in theology, "Yeah, I guess I'll be tired, but since I won't be meeting my husband's needs (wink wink) on those twelve nights, I imagine it will sort of balance out." If I had reached over and spooned out a portion of his peach melba, he could not have been more shocked. To say nothing of my husband.

But if my humiliation was dramatic in content, it was, at least, limited in scope. Only the tall, and now pale, theologian, my shaken husband, and I were aware of my faux pas. Next up was Dave's wife.

With dessert under way, the president began his presidential duties—making a speech and then making the rounds. "Ding, ding, ding," chimed his silver spoon on his crystal goblet, and the room immediately fell silent. "I would just like to say", the president began, "that this university could not, would not, be an institution of excellence without the dedication and brilliance of its faculty." There was more. We were all prepared for more. But Dave's wife, either overcome by the peach melba or by her husband's success, temporarily lost her mind. "Woo hoo!" she screamed, in the fashion of someone attending an athletic event. "Woo hoo!" she repeated and then pumped her fist in the air. We could not have been more startled if she had pulled an air horn from her purse. The president too was startled, so much so that he lost his balance, and his champagne, intended for the imminent toast, swirled around on the inside of his fluted glass. But you do not get appointed president of a university for want of verbal agility, and with only the slightest awkward delay, he added, "and, of course, faculty spouses." Here, here.

Relieved that the theologian was no longer looking at me, I followed his eyes and saw Dave's wife sink into her chair, the back of her neck flaming red, her head tilted to one side as if trying to make sense of what just happened. But, as acute as Dave's wife's agony was, it would prove to be short-lived. As the president continued his toast, another spousal humiliation was brewing.

Elena, a history professor seated at our table, had recently been promoted to the dual roles of associate professor and mother. Through the salad and main course, her baby boy rested behind her in his stroller while Elena and her husband, Liam, dined. By dessert, though, baby Owen was no longer content to sit, preferring, instead, to be bounced in his father's arms. So as not to disrupt the president's speech, Liam carried Owen silently out of the dining room while the president completed his toast. Following polite and predictable applause, the president did something unpredictable. He announced a birthday, raised a glass, offered a second toast, and then led us all in singing "Happy Birthday" to a very embarrassed professor of psychology.

Singing "Happy Birthday" to anyone can be embarrassing. Both the singers and the singee are aware of a shift in the room, a sort of "all eyes on me" thing that psychologists tell us makes us deeply uncomfortable.

If the awkwardness is somewhat abated when singing to a gleeful child, it is all the more pronounced when singing to a self-conscious adult. It is hard to know where to look (if you are ever singing to me, may I suggest looking anywhere but at me) and even harder to know which name to use. "Happy birthday, dear Dr. Stevens/Regina/Reggie/sweetheart ... Happy forty-seventh birthday to you!" Still, with the help of the president, we, and Dr. Stevens, survived the salute and quickly went back to our dessert.

Enter Liam. With baby Owen now settled, Liam seated himself between his wife and Dr. Stevens just in time to see a special dessert, topped with a sputtering little candle, be presented to the doctor. "What's this?" he asked. And in quiet tones Dr. Stevens admitted that it was her birthday. "Well then", beamed Liam, and he stood, raising both arms in a gesture of beckoning, and burst forth with, "Happy birthday to ..."

But we could not do it—no one, not even the president, joined in. Liam, arms still held high, looked around the room, confused. Dr. Stevens swallowed, held onto the edge of the table, and stared resolutely into her lap. Elena hissed, "Sit down." Liam sank into his chair and, looking at me, mouthed the words, "What did I do?" "Don't worry about it", I whispered back. "It was just one extra thing too many."

It is not just professors and their spouses who have irreconcilable differences. All couples have moments when they are not feeling united and do not even want to feel united.

The difference between happy couples and those who are not happy is not irreconcilable differences but rather how they deal with those differences. As marital psychologists Scott M. Stanley, Susan L. Blumberg, and Howard J. Markman point out in their book *Fighting for Your Marriage*, "Twenty-five years of research tell us that success in marriage is related not so much to the nature of the differences between the two partners as to how the partners handle the differences they have."[9] How then should such differences be handled?

The two best resources of which I am aware for couples are the books *Fighting for Your Marriage* and John Gottman's *Seven Principles for Making Marriage Work*.[10] Both are based on decades of empirical research about what helps couples succeed and what couples should avoid in order to make their relationships work. Rather than attempting to summarize them, I strongly recommend reading and taking to heart the empirically verified recommendations of these books.

Forgiveness

As both of the aforementioned books recognize, a key aspect of covenant marriage is forgiveness. In any long-term relationship, whether it is a marital relationship, a deep friendship, a family bond, or simply a relationship with a coworker, trouble will arise at one time or another.

[9] Scott M. Stanley, Susan L. Blumberg, and Howard J. Markman, *Fighting for Your Marriage* (San Francisco: Jossey-Bass, 2001), 27.

[10] John Gottman, *Seven Principles for Making Marriage Work* (New York: Three Rivers, 1999).

No two human beings can go long without disagreements, misunderstandings, misinterpretations, and hurt feelings. A choice ultimately will arise: either forgive the other person or hold on to the hurt.

Researchers in positive psychology, such as Christopher Peterson at the University of Michigan, have found that forgiveness is a trait that is necessary for happiness. In order to be happy, human beings need close relationships with others that last. Since all long-term relationships sooner or later have some kind of difficulty, forgiveness is necessary in order to preserve these relationships. The equation is simple: No forgiveness, no good long-term relationships; no good long-term relationships, no deep-lasting (level three, level four) happiness.

What exactly is forgiveness? Many people think that forgiveness means forgetting about an offense that happened. This is not true. Painful memories can be almost impossible to forget. Forgiveness is not properly understood as getting amnesia about what happened.

Nor is forgiveness an emotion, or feeling better about what happened. If someone does something horrible to you—say, kills your brother or sister—you will always feel pain about the loss. Your emotions toward the killer will likely always be affected by what was done. Forgiveness does not mean feeling as if everything is wonderful.

Nor is forgiveness pretending as if nothing happened. If a person is an ongoing threat, then that person should be avoided and, if needed, legally restrained. Taking such action is compatible with forgiveness and love. Love seeks what is good for the beloved, and enabling evil behavior is not good for the beloved.

Nor is forgiveness saying that nothing wrong was done. If wrong was done, it would be a lie to say that nothing wrong was done.

What then is forgiveness? Forgiveness is a choice, a decision. Forgiveness takes place when the offended party chooses to release the guilty party from owing a debt of guilt. Forgiveness is the decision to let go of plotting revenge and instead to pardon the wrongdoer. Ideally, forgiveness follows repentance by the guilty party, when he has a change of heart and changes his ways, typically manifested by admitting wrongdoing and asking for forgiveness. However, it is possible to forgive someone who has not admitted wrongdoing. For example, you can forgive a person who has died or someone who fails to see that he has done wrong against you. In the best situation, the people involved can achieve reconciliation. Reconciliation is the restoration of trust that takes place when the guilty repent, the offended forgive, and the relationship of trust is restored.

How often should a person choose to forgive? The answer to this question depends upon one's philosophy and theology. From a level one perspective, a person should forgive if it helps the person to get more bodily pleasure. From a level two perspective, a person should forgive so long as it will help in the pursuit of level two goods. From a level three perspective—since level three is about loving all human beings, both oneself and the person who has done wrong—a person should forgive every human being who needs it, both for the sake of those human beings and for the sake of the one who is doing the forgiving, so that the offended party can set down the burden of fostering anger and seeking revenge.

From a level four perspective, a person should forgive as often as God forgives. The understanding of God given by Jesus emphasizes the importance of forgiveness. Jesus taught his followers to pray, "Forgive us our trespasses, / As we forgive those who trespass against us" (Mt 6:12). Jesus emphasized the unlimited scope of forgiveness. "Peter came up and said to him [Jesus], 'Lord, how often shall my brother sin against me, and I forgive him? As many as seven times?' Jesus said to him, 'I do not say to you seven times, but seventy times seven'" (Mt 18:21–22). Jesus does not mean that after you forgive someone 490 times, the offending person is out of luck. "Seventy times seven" is a poetic way of saying, "Forgive perfectly, without limit." Jesus said that failure to forgive undermines our own relationship with God: "If you forgive men their trespasses, your heavenly Father also will forgive you; but if you do not forgive men their trespasses, neither will your Father forgive your trespasses" (Mt 6:14–16). So from a level four perspective, at least as Jesus understood it, forgiveness is absolutely essential for happiness. The promise to love one's spouse includes forgiving one's spouse, even for catastrophically horrible crimes.

Fulfilling the Marriage Vow in the Worst-Case Scenario

When I speak to students about the nature of covenant marriage, about the commitment I have undertaken, they invariably ask a version of the following question: "So, you are saying that you will not divorce your wife and marry somebody else, no matter what? What if your wife commits adultery? What if she develops a drinking problem or starts abusing drugs? What if she goes crazy and murders your children and tries to murder you?"

Well, I certainly do hope that none of those horrible things happen. I also hope that if those horrible things do happen that I have the courage and the fortitude to carry out the commitment that I made. I promised to love Jennifer as my spouse until death do us part. "Until death do us part" means exactly what it says: until death do us part. If the worst-case scenario took place, I would still have an obligation to love Jennifer, as my spouse, unconditionally.

What does this commitment look like in the doomsday scenario? If I came home and found all the kids dead and found my wife coming after me with a bloody knife in her hand, I would get away as quickly as I could. I would then call the police to report the entire incident. None of this contradicts the solemn marriage vow. To love someone does not mean that one must become a victim to another's criminal and immoral activity. Indeed, real love desires what is good for the person, not to enable someone's bad behavior. So if my wife became a crazed serial killer, I would try to get her the help that she desperately needed. I would help the police to lock her up so that she could not harm herself or others and so that she could get psychiatric treatment. Notice that in the marriage vow there is no promise made to live with the other person every day of your life. In difficult scenarios, like the one mentioned above, it is necessary to live separately from the abusive or mentally ill spouse, as it would be necessary to live apart from an abusive or mentally ill child, brother, sister, or parent. In some cases, this separation will have a salutary effect in helping the abusing person come to the realization that offensive, immoral, and illegal behavior needs to stop. In other cases, it is simply making the best of a horrible situation.

If the worst-case scenario happened to me, of course, I would be devastated. My wife is my best friend, and if she were in prison or in a psych ward, I can hardly imagine how horrible it would be. In many respects, my life would be ruined, and it is unlikely that I would ever fully recover.

Yet with time, I hope that I would at least partially recover. Happiness, as noted in the introduction, has many dimensions. If I am faithful to my vows, my level one happiness, in terms of sex, would be over, since with my spouse permanently locked up, it would be infidelity to begin a sexual relationship with someone else. But my level one happiness in other respects would still be possible. I could still eat double-double burgers from In-N-Out, I could still enjoy cool Corona beer, and I could still run with my iPod. In the worst-case scenario, my level two happiness would also be significantly undermined because I would be humiliated and embarrassed by what had happened and by the whispers (not entirely without justification) that I had driven my wife over the edge of sanity. My social position would also be seriously undermined in many ways, not least of which I would presumably no longer be invited to events for couples. But even my level two happiness would not be entirely abolished. I could still try to get raises at work and seek other accomplishments of a level two kind. What about level three? Well, as long as I have the power to choose, no one can destroy my level three happiness. The choice to love or not to love other people remains even in the most difficult of circumstances. In a similar way, level four happiness, a loving relationship with God, cannot be destroyed by anyone else's actions. Indeed, in being faithful to what I promised in the marriage vow, I would be providing powerful witness to others and serving God with a kind of white martyrdom where no blood is shed but the suffering is severe nonetheless. In depression and despair, I might undermine my own level three and level four happiness, but that would be my own action and not the actions of my wife or anyone else. Obviously, I hope that such a marital catastrophe never happens to me (or to anyone else), but if it did happen, it would not mean the end of all meaning and happiness in life.

I have a dear friend who did go through a version of the worst-case scenario. Her husband committed adultery, secretly taped himself and the woman having sex for a friend to watch, and betrayed his country and caused people to die in what was called the worst intelligence disaster in U.S. history. He is now serving life without parole in a supermax prison that holds a convicted 9/11 terrorist and the Unabomber and that held Timothy McVeigh before his execution. After this man's sentencing, after all details of his crimes and immoral behavior were made public, my friend was asked whether she would divorce her husband. She replied, "I'll never divorce him. I love him, and I'll pray for the salvation of his soul every day for the rest of my life." One might imagine that my friend is miserable. I think I would be destroyed by what she went through. The truth is, she is one of the happiest people I know.

The Third Big Myth

"Love Alone Makes a Marriage"

*The Reality: More than love is needed
to create a covenant marriage.*

The question, what is marriage? is controversial today. Across the United States, politicians, lawyers, and pundits debate the legalization of same-sex marriage. Some professors, pundits, and polygamists argue that it is a form of bigotry to limit marriage only to two people, excluding unions of any number of people. Jillian Keenan, in her *Slate* article "Legalize Polygamy! No, I Am Not Kidding", argues that marriage is "plastic", that is, whatever legal, consenting adults want it to be.[1] The media has publicized even less common "marriages". Dennis Rodman married himself, and Nadine Schweigert married herself. The online encyclopedia Wikipedia lists marriages of humans to dogs, snakes, cows, horses, and goats. Babylonia Aivaz, a woman from Seattle, married a 107-year-old warehouse on Capitol Hill. After the building was destroyed, she

---

[1] Jillian Keenan, "Legalize Polygamy! No. I Am Not Kidding", *Slate*, April 15, 2013, http://www.slate.com/articles/double_x/doublex/2013/04/legalize_polygamy_marriage_equality_for_all.html.

announced her engagement to a Seattle neighborhood. No one seemed to question why a widow should move so quickly to engagement with another.

Like any word, "marriage" must be defined because, if marriage means anything and everything, then marriage means nothing. Abraham Lincoln is purported to have said, "How many legs does a dog have if you call the tail a leg? Four. Calling a tail a leg doesn't make it a leg." Similarly, people can call whatever they want "marriage", but calling such arrangements marriages does not make them marriages. This chapter considers the question of what kinds of unions can be covenant marriages. It looks at the idea of annulment of marriage to enable a better understanding of what marriage is before considering whether various kinds of unions could possibly be covenant marriages.

But first a word about what marriage is not. Judge Vaughn Walker, who struck down California's Proposition 8 reserving marriage for one man and one woman, defined marriage as follows: "Marriage is the state recognition and approval of a couple's choice to live with each other, to remain committed to one another and to form a household based on their own feelings about one another and to join in an economic partnership and support one another and any dependents."[2]

This definition surely cannot be correct. Marriage does not necessarily involve a couple's choice to live together, since a couple who get married just prior to the military deployment of one of them are choosing to get married

---

[2] Ruling by United States District Court, *Perry v. Schwarzenegger* (2010), 67. Available online at the Scribd digital library, http://www.scribd.com /doc/35374462/California-Prop-8-Ruling-August-2010.

but are not choosing to live together. Nor does legal marriage (at least in the United States) involve the choice "to remain committed to one another". Countless marriages fail to have commitment, as numerous cases including divorce and infidelity make clear. Nor again does marriage necessarily involve forming "a household based on [the couple's] own feelings about one another". In some cases, couples choose to marry based on their feelings about one another, but other couples choose to marry based on convenience, greed, religious conviction, financial arrangement, or just plain animal lust. The last part of Walker's definition is also erroneous: "to join in an economic partnership and support one another and any dependents". Some marriages are indeed economic partnerships of shared property and cash, but other marriages have strict division and separation of all economic resources. Similarly, some spouses support one another in various ways, while others do not. Some married couples have and support dependents, while others do not. Walker's definition of marriage is deeply flawed.

Let us turn to something that is perhaps common ground. If anything is a marriage, covenant marriage is a marriage. If that is not a marriage, then nothing is a marriage. Covenant marriage is the paradigm case. But not everyone who walks down the aisle and repeats the words of the covenant marriage vow has entered into a covenant marriage. Some of these ceremonies do not result in marriage at all and so are subject to annulment. Indeed, annulment clarifies to a degree the nature of marriage.

What is annulment? Annulment is not divorce for a covenant marriage. Rather, annulment is a declaration that there was no covenant marriage from the very beginning. Saying the words of the covenant marriage vow—even when wearing a tuxedo, in front of a religious minister or judge, and before family and friends—is not enough to enter a covenant marriage. For example, two small children, even if they repeat the vows of a covenant marriage, are not married, since they are too young to be able to give consent to any serious matter, let alone consent to something as significant as lifelong marriage. Likewise, some adults (either permanently or temporarily) have minds that are no more capable of giving consent than are the minds of small children. So even if such an adult were to say the covenant marriage vows, that adult has not entered into a covenant marriage since no free consent was given.

For example, imagine that the daughter of a Mafia boss is with child. The don comes to the young man who got his daughter pregnant and says, "You had better marry my daughter a month from this Saturday, or I am going to make sure you have a little accident and sleep with the fishes." If this man gets married under threat of death, he may say the vows and may give consent, but since his consent is not free but coerced, no covenant marriage has been created (even if the woman gives her free consent). Covenant marriage is a gift of one person to another as spouse, and in order for the gift of the self to be considered as such, it must be freely given rather than forced. A union created under violent duress is not a covenant marriage and so can be annulled. A person's free choice to be united to another can never—by definition—be compelled against the person's will. Without being united in will, the couple cannot be comprehensively united.

Another case of a union that may be annulled occurs when one party (or both) takes the marriage vow in bad faith. If someone takes the marriage vow but has no intention of actually carrying out that vow, no covenant marriage has been created. Imagine a case in which a man wants to marry a rich heiress simply to get her money, and on the night before the wedding he tells a group of friends, "I really fooled her. All I have to do is stick it out for one year and then divorce her. My attorney says I'll get three million in the settlement easily." The next day, the man says the covenant marriage vow, but he is merely saying words without any intention of carrying out what those words mean. He is like the man who swears in court to "tell the truth, the whole truth, and nothing but the truth" knowing that he will lie and perjure himself. People who swear the oath of covenant marriage in bad faith have not entered into a covenant marriage because they have not chosen to give themselves to their spouse but have chosen to lie and misrepresent themselves instead.

Annulments can take place for a variety of reasons, including but not limited to the examples given. What all instances of justifiable annulment share is a focus on when a couple weds. In such instances, the conditions necessary for a true marriage were simply not met at the time of the wedding. If either party was unable to wed because of lack of sufficient age and maturity, then no covenant marriage was created. If either party did not freely consent to marriage because he was forced to marry, the couple have not entered into a covenant marriage. If either party (or both) intentionally lied when taking the marriage vows and never intended to enter a covenant marriage, then what appeared to be a covenant marriage in fact was never a covenant marriage. In all these cases, an apparent covenant marriage can be annulled.

Annulment is a declaration that what appeared to be a covenant marriage was in reality not a covenant marriage. This declaration regards the circumstances surrounding when the union began, not about what happened five, ten, or thirty years later. It is sometimes confusing to think that a couple who went through a covenant marriage ceremony could be together for years or even decades and yet not be in a covenant marriage. To illustrate a similar idea, imagine a married couple returning from the hospital after the mother has given birth to a baby boy. They are delighted. They have a wonderful little family together, and as the years pass, the love of all three deepens. Unfortunately, when the boy is nineteen, he develops a strange health condition. The father takes him to the doctor, and the doctor informs them that this genetic condition is passed from father to son and never through the mother. Since the father has never had any symptoms of this strange health condition, a team of doctors thoroughly examines him. The doctors discover the father is entirely free of his son's malady. Further DNA testing reveals that the man is not the biological father of this teenage boy, although the man has been raising him as a son for nineteen years. Now, the man obviously is the father of the boy in many senses—he raised the boy; he loves him as a son; the mother might even have thought that her husband was the biological father. Yet the man is not the biological father. Biological fatherhood was determined at the boy's conception, and nothing that happened later, good or bad, could change this fact.

In a similar way, a couple married for many years were obviously married in some real sense. That they were indeed married is not in question, and that is why any children born of such a marital union are not illegitimate. The question is whether the couple had a covenant marriage, which they either had or did not have from the day of their wedding. In a case in which a marriage is annulled, the answer is that they did not in fact have a covenant marriage from the conception of their marriage. Consequently, both parties are still free to enter into a covenant marriage.

What Kinds of Unions Can Be Covenant Marriages?

The possibility of annulment makes clear that simply going through a covenant marriage ceremony is not sufficient for creating a covenant marriage. Two toddlers can repeat any kind of words they like, including marriage vows, but they simply cannot get married due to their immaturity. Given that there are many, many different kinds of things that people call marriages, let us consider whether those various arrangements would constitute a covenant marriage.

The exchange of vows is needed to create a covenant marriage, so in any case in which vows are not exchanged, there can be no covenant marriage. Thus, neither a building nor animals can enter a covenant marriage. Likewise, anyone who cannot communicate free and informed consent to a marital union cannot get married. The creation of a covenant marriage requires that those who enter into it be able to give themselves in a complete way to one another in a mutual exchange as spouses. Anyone who is incapable of making such a mutual free exchange—such as children, mentally incompetent adults, inanimate objects, and animals—cannot enter a covenant marriage. They cannot have a comprehensive marital relationship, since they are incapable of understanding and committing to giving themselves as spouses to each other until death do they part.

Polygamy

Could there be covenant marriage between one man and several women, one woman and several men, or any number of humans beyond two, for example, five men and three women? In other words, could there be such a thing as a polygamous covenant marriage?

In the course of history, approximately 85 percent of societies have practiced polygamy. Pushed by advocates of same-sex marriage and multiculturalism, some scholars, such as the signers of the statement "Beyond Same-Sex Marriage", argue that it is irrational and bigoted for contemporary society to limit marriage to couples.

However, treating different things differently is not bigotry, and there are many important differences between polygamy and monogamy in practice as well as in principle. Let us begin with the practical considerations drawn from human experience. Empirically speaking, in virtually every respect, polygamy is socially detrimental—to society in general, to men, to women, and to children. These problems arise because of the nature of human reproduction.

In human reproduction, slightly more male than female babies are born (approximately 105 boys to 100 girls). Boys are more likely to die of natural causes as infants and from violence before they marry and reproduce. So other things being equal, at any given marriageable age, there will be approximately 50 percent males and 50 percent females. Given roughly equal numbers of males and females as found in nature, polygamy and monogamy shape society in radically different ways.

In polygyny, by far the most common form of polygamy, one man may marry a number of wives. In polyandry, one wife has two or more husbands. This latter form of polygamy is extremely unusual in societies and often takes the form of two brothers marrying the same woman. In polygynandry, two or more wives marry two or more husbands. Polygynandry is even rarer than polyandry but is similar in some respects to polygyny, insofar as a man has more than one wife. Since both polygynandry and polyandry are virtually nonexistent in societies, I will focus on the more common case of one man with multiple wives and will use the term "polygamy" to describe this marital arrangement.

Imagine a society of two hundred people. In a monogamous society, there would be one man for each woman. In a polygamous society, this one-to-one ratio does not hold. What typically happens in polygamous society is that the wealthiest men have more than one wife. So in the society we are describing, the two wealthiest men have ten wives each; the next-wealthiest man has eight wives; the three next-wealthiest men have four wives each; and the five next-wealthiest men have two wives each. Therefore, the ten richest men have fifty wives in total among them, leaving ninety poorer men to compete for the attention of the fifty remaining single women. Even if the remaining men seek only one wife each, forty men will have no wives at all. What social effects does this arrangement bring?

Joseph Henrich, Robert Boyd, and Peter J. Richerson, in their article "The Puzzle of Monogamous Marriage", use converging lines of evidences from the social sciences to compare polygamous and monogamous societies.[3] They found that polygamous societies differ from monogamous societies in terms of violent crimes, female educational attainment, domestic violence, parental investment in children, and economic productivity.

A wealth of sociological information points to the fact that single men commit the vast majority of violent crimes. Women and married men tend to have very low rates of murder, robbery, rape, and assault by comparison. So, since there are many more single men in polygamous societies, polygamous societies have higher rates of violent crime. As Henrich and colleagues note, "Faced with high levels of intra-sexual competition and little chance of obtaining even one long-term mate, unmarried, low-status men will heavily discount the future and more readily engage in risky status-elevating and sex-seeking behaviours. This will result in higher rates of murder, theft, rape, social disruption, kidnapping (especially of females), sexual slavery

[3] Joseph Henrich, Robert Boyd, and Peter J. Richerson, "The Puzzle of Monogamous Marriage", *Philosophical Transactions of the Royal Society of London*, series B: Biological Sciences, 367, no. 1589 (2012): 657–69, doi:10.1098/rstb.2011.0290. Data supplement: http://rstb.royalsocietypublishing.org/content/367/1589/657/suppl/DC1.

and prostitution."[4] With little reason to invest in the established social order, single males are more likely to turn away from activities conducive to long-term productivity and turn toward the quick thrill, if not violent overthrow of the established social order. Obviously, these tendencies are detrimental to society as a whole.

In a polygamous society, the age of marriage is lower for females than it is in a monogamous society, note Henrich and colleagues. With a relative scarcity of possible mates of the same age, men seek wives among women of younger ages. Early marriage in turn leads to much higher rates of reproduction. Females, rather than delaying marrying and having babies in their twenties or thirties, marry and have children as teenagers. In modern social conditions, teen motherhood is detrimental for both these young women and their families. For a female teen, marriage to a much older man makes it unlikely that she will have an equal partnership with her husband and makes the completion of her education difficult if not impossible. Indeed, marriage at a young age to a much older man is also linked to lethal domestic violence: "The larger the age gap, the more likely it is that a husband will kill his wife, and vice-versa (the young wife murders her husband).... This suggests that polygyny is relatively (potentially) much more dangerous than monogamous relations because age gaps of 16 years are not uncommon when accumulating young wives."[5] The difference in age is more likely to give rise to jealous fears in older men that their young wives will be unfaithful.

[4] Ibid., 660.
[5] Ibid., data supplement, 25.

The phenomenon of "co-wives" (a misnomer because polygamy typically involves a hierarchy among the wives) also undermines the well-being of women. The senior wives worry that they will be replaced by younger wives, and the younger wives worry about the power exerted in the home by senior wives. Research indicates that levels of domestic strife and violence are higher in polygamous homes than in monogamous homes, as wives seek to preserve their place with their shared husband as well as struggle to secure resources for their own biological children. As Henrich and colleagues point out, "Co-wife conflict is ubiquitous in polygynous households. From anthropology, a review of ethnographic data from 69 non-sororal [i.e., wives who are not sisters] polygynous societies from around the globe reveals no case where co-wife relations could be described as harmonious, and no hint that women's access to the means of production [i.e., women working in industrial societies] had any mitigating impact on conflict."[6] These conflicts lead polygamous family units to have higher rates of divorce than monogamous couples.

If polygamy is bad for women, it is perhaps even worse for the well-being of children. Because the polygamous wives tend to be very young and less well educated than monogamous wives, their children suffer from having less mature mothers. The children suffer also from having multiple stepmothers involved in ongoing struggles with each other. Half siblings must compete for limited resources while having weaker genetic bonds, that is, full

[6] Ibid., 665.

siblings have more to bond them together than do half siblings. While these extended family relationships could in theory be a source of support, more often they endanger children. Henrich's study found that

> much empirical work in monogamous societies indicates that higher degrees of relatedness among household members are associated with lower rates of abuse, neglect and homicide. Living in the same household with genetically unrelated adults is the single biggest risk factor for abuse, neglect and homicide of children. Stepmothers are 2.4 times more likely to kill their stepchildren than birth mothers, and children living with an unrelated parent are between 15 and 77 times more likely to die "accidentally."[7]

Polygamous families are also more likely than monogamous families to be in poverty, since typically only one breadwinner supports more children than any monogamous family could have.

Polygamous societies also dilute the investment of fathers in their children in at least two ways. First, because marriage to other young women is still an option, a husband's resources of time, attention, and money are diverted away from his own children and toward finding new wives. Second, since countless polygamous families have many more children than any monogamous couple could ever have, it becomes increasingly difficult for a father to give each child sufficient time and attention. For example, Mohammed bin Laden, the father of Osama bin Laden, had some fifty-eight children with his multiple wives. Indeed, some

[7] Ibid.

fathers of polygamous families have so many children that they do not even know each child's name. This dilution of paternal investment is in effect similar to a child being raised by a single mother, with all the attendant risk factors (especially for males) for abusing drugs, breaking the law, and dropping out of school.

A final harm brought by polygamy—on men, women, and children—is economic hardship. Henrich's study notes, "When males cannot invest in obtaining more wives (because of imposed monogamy) they invest and save in ways that generate both reduced population growth and more rapid economic expansion (increasing GDP [gross domestic product] per capita). Thus, ... the nearly three-fold increase in GDP per capita between Comparable Monogamous Countries and Highly Polygynous Countries is partially caused by legally imposed monogamy."[8] Economic well-being contributes in turn to the stability of families, which is a benefit to men, women, and children.

Finally, putting aside sociological data, we can ask an important question. Could a polygamous union be a covenant marriage? One aspect of covenant marriage could be present in a polygamous relationship, namely, unconditional love. It is possible to promise more than one person that you will love him unconditionally. Good parents have unconditional love for however many sons and daughters they may have, and this parental relationship can also be created by choice, as in the case of adoption. Therefore, one man could promise unconditional love for all his wives and vow never to divorce any of them.

[8] Ibid., data supplement, 16.

However, covenant marriage includes more than just the promise of unconditional love. In a covenant marriage, spouses give themselves as spouses to each other unreservedly, unconditionally, and entirely. Part of the marriage vow is the promise of sexual fidelity, the bodily manifestation of one's commitment as spouse entirely to the spouse and to the spouse alone. Polygamous relationships cannot be covenant marriages of mutual and complete self-donation as spouses, since it is intrinsically impossible to reserve oneself in a sexual way entirely for one person and at the same time reserve oneself in a sexual way entirely for a different person. And since it makes no sense to promise what is logically impossible, one cannot have a covenant marriage with two people at the same time. A covenant marriage can therefore exist only between two persons, and never between more than two persons.

Furthermore, polygamous marriage involves an inherent inequality and a gender hierarchy that render these kinds of unions incapable of being covenant marriages. In a polygamous marriage, the man does not give himself qua husband entirely to one wife. A polygamous husband gives himself qua husband to however many wives he has. However, the wives are expected to reserve themselves in a sexual way for their husband alone. Polygamous marriage is therefore inherently unequal. On the basis of the equality between husband and wife and their friendship, Saint Thomas Aquinas rejects polygamy:

> Friendship consists in an equality. So, if it is not lawful for the wife to have several husbands, since this is contrary to the certainty of offspring, it would not be

lawful, on the other hand, for a man to have several wives, for the friendship of wife for husband would not be free but somewhat servile. And this argument is corroborated by experience, for among husbands having plural wives the wives have a status like that of servants. Furthermore, strong friendship is not possible in regard for many people, as is evident from the Philosopher [Aristotle] in *Ethics* VIII. Therefore, if a wife has but one husband, but the husband has several wives, the friendship will not be equal on both sides.[9]

Not only are the wives not equal to their husband, but characteristically the wives are not even equal among themselves, as "senior wives" enjoy rank above "junior wives".

Self-Marriage

A polygamous marriage cannot be a covenant marriage, but can self-marriage be a covenant marriage? Just as a covenant marriage cannot exist for more than two people, so too it cannot exist with less than two people. A person can and should love himself by choosing what is truly good for himself, because every human person, including oneself, should be loved unconditionally. But spousal love is not identical to self-love. One cannot "give" oneself in words and in body to oneself, since each person already possesses himself. Indeed, the very idea of covenant marriage presupposes that each person may make a gift of

[9] Thomas Aquinas, *Summa contra Gentiles*, trans. Vernon J. Bourke (Notre Dame, Ind.: University of Notre Dame Press, 1975), III, ch. 124, nn. 4 and 5, p. 152.

himself to the other, for one cannot licitly give away what one does not have authority to give away. In like manner, one cannot receive what one already possesses, so no man can receive himself as a gift from himself. So Dennis Rodman (or Nadine Schweigert) cannot create a covenant marriage to himself (or to herself). An individual can go through whatever ceremony he likes, and say whatever words he likes, but no covenant marriage can be created by one person alone.

Same-Sex Marriage

Can covenant marriage exist between two men or between two women, or must it exist only between one man and one woman? Couples of the same sex can certainly manifest aspects of the covenant marriage vow. They can commit to each other in the words of a covenant marriage: in good times and in bad, in sickness and in health, until death do they part. They can have agape in a totally unreserved and unconditional sense. They can be faithful to each other and reserve themselves sexually only for their spouse alone, forsaking all others. They can certainly love each other in all the senses of love—eros, philia, and agape.

Part of creating a covenant marriage is the verbal oath that the couple takes, so as noted earlier, whoever is incapable or unwilling to make a covenant oath cannot be in a covenant marriage. This verbal oath can be taken and honored by a same-sex couple just as by an opposite-sex couple. But another part of creating an indissoluble covenant marriage is the bodily consent to the union, called in civil and in canon law the consummation of the marriage. Marriage is not merely a union of wills or of minds, because marriage is a union of human persons, who are always embodied. The couple who exchange marriage vows have united themselves in will and in mind to be spouses, but they must also unite themselves in body to be fully united as married human persons.

Human beings can be united in body in various ways. A couple could shake hands, and this unites them in a bodily way. Yet shaking hands is a rather superficial way to be united. The way of bodily uniting that expresses the maximal commitment of covenant marriage is not merely the shaking of hands, or hugging, or even kissing. These ways of uniting physically, through increasing levels of intimacy and unity, do not express the deepest kind of unity of which human beings are capable.

What kind of physical unity reflects the maximal character of the marriage vow? The obvious answer is a sexual unity. This answer also makes sense of why faithful spouses reserve sex for each other alone but may shake hands with, hug, or embrace others. Now, like other kinds of bodily contact, sexual contact itself is not simply of one kind but varies in terms of its intimacy and depth. Teenagers still speak of "first base"—kissing passionately; "second base"—fondling; "third base"—genital manipulation and oral sex; and a "home run"—sexual intercourse. To "go all the way" means to have sexual intercourse.

Only a man and a woman can "go all the way". They become united not simply in terms of enjoying each other in a sexual way, for this takes place at all levels of sexual contact. They are united in body by engaging in the kind of act that is ordered to procreation (whether or not they actually procreate). The male and female sex organs, bodily dimensions of the human persons, are not merely rubbing together but are actually working together and united for a shared goal of procreation (even if this shared goal is not reached or is not consciously desired). Indeed, this openness to procreation differentiates sexual intercourse even among male-female couples. To have sex with someone knowing that procreation is a real possibility, without using contraception, is to give oneself to that person in a fuller way than to have sex in which contraception is used and in which procreation (the fullest union possible of male and female on the biological level) is intentionally excluded.

Because covenant marriage unites human persons, who are both intellectual and embodied beings, it must unite them both in mind and in body. Any couple who are, in principle, incapable of giving themselves fully to each other in terms of mind and will are incapable of entering a covenant marriage. Similarly, any couple who cannot become united in the most comprehensive bodily way are incapable of entering a covenant marriage. Covenant marriage is, therefore, reserved for one man and one woman.

If this analysis is correct, then covenant marriage can only exist between one man and one woman. It must be a man and a woman and not a boy and a girl because boys and girls are not capable of giving free informed consent to a lifelong commitment as spouses. It must be *one* man and *one* woman because polygamous spouses do not give themselves as spouses entirely and unreservedly to their spouse and their spouse alone. It must be one *man* and one *woman* because two men or two women are not able to maximally unite in a bodily way that reflects the full consent to be spouses given in the marital vow.

The most common alternative to covenant marriage is not polygamy, self-marriage, or same-sex marriage. The most common alternative to covenant marriage is cohabitation, or living together without marriage. It is that subject to which we now turn.

The Fourth Big Myth

"Cohabitation Is Just Like Marriage"

*The Reality: Marriage is unlike cohabitation
in practice and in principle.*

"Should we live together?" Some romantic couples choose
to cohabit as a stage on the way to marriage or simply as
an alternative to marriage. Although some people cohabit
with no intention of ever getting married, most who
cohabit plan to marry at some point. Even some people
who do not cohabit approve of the practice and view it as
an important stage in a romantic relationship in which the
couple figure out whether they really get along. The question for the generous person is, would a virtuous person
choose to cohabit?

Following family researcher Glenn Stanton, we can distinguish two different ways in which marriage and cohabitation are related.[1] Some couples choose cohabitation
in part because they have a low view of marriage, while
other couples choose it because they have a high view of
marriage.

[1] Glenn Stanton, *Why Marriage Matters: Reasons to Believe in Marriage in Post-
modern Society* (Colorado Springs, Colo.: NavPress, 1997), 55–56.

Individuals who have a low view of marriage do not think that matrimony is very important. Marriage, for them, is just a piece of paper, a formality and legality that is irrelevant. Happiness, cooperation, communication, trust, love, and commitment are what matter in a relationship—not legalities. Matrimony, in this view, makes no difference in terms of the warmth, love, satisfaction, and joy of the relationship. While some feel simply neutral toward marriage, believing it will not help or hinder their relationship, others view marriage as detrimental to their relationship. Glenn Stanton describes this view:

> To become legally married would weigh down a beautiful and unencumbered love with the ugly legalities of a business contract. Such baggage would only serve to choke out the lifeblood of the relationship. Does love require a legal document to legitimize itself? Without such entanglements, two people could remain together because they desire to be together, not because some legal entity says they must. Cohabitation would allow the warmth of love, not cold legalities, to regulate the temperature of domestic relationships.[2]

In the low view of marriage, people are seen as staying together out of love, not because of some legal agreement. After all, couples will either stay together or they will not; a marriage license will not change anything.

By contrast, supporters of cohabitation who have a high view of marriage think that marriage is vitally important rather than just a piece of paper. In the high view, marriage is so important, and divorce so devastating, that you

[2] Ibid., 56.

had better be as sure as possible that you have chosen the right person to marry. The best way to do this is by cohabitation. By living together before a possible wedding, you can evaluate whether or not marriage to this person would be a good idea. Cohabitation is seen as an ideal testing ground to see whether or not you really love someone and whether this someone really loves you. Living together is a perfect way to winnow out partners who are incompatible so as to find "the one". If the cohabiting relationship does not work out, then the two individuals can seek out other people with whom they are more compatible. People with the high view of marriage deeply desire to live a happy life as husband and wife, and so in order to increase the likelihood of this happening, they move in together with the intention of reducing the likelihood of divorce.

In a feat of logical gymnastics, sometimes individuals offer both the low view of marriage and the high view of marriage as justifications for cohabitation. In one breath, a person might say, "Marriage is so important that you shouldn't rush into it without prior experience living together", but in the next breath, the person claims, "Marriage doesn't really matter anyway." These views are not consistent. But much more than inconsistency leads opponents of cohabitation to be down on shacking up.

Cohabitation and the Low View of Marriage

Let us examine the low view first. In the low view, matrimony does not matter; what matters is the quality of the relationship. When a couple cohabit, they are free from the burdens of the institution of marriage, and so their relationship can flourish much more than within the confines of a legally recognized partnership.

But do intimate relationships typically flourish more in cohabitation than in marriage? The evidence points overwhelmingly to the conclusion that they do not. Compared with married couples, cohabiting couples have more disagreements, more domestic violence, more infidelity, more abuse of alcohol and drugs, and more breakups.[3] Married couples report higher levels of sexual satisfaction, better communication with each other, greater physical and mental well-being, a more equal distribution of domestic chores, and higher levels of happiness.[4] Although many people believe that cohabitors are no different from spouses or even that cohabitation is superior to marriage, decades of research controlling for race and economic status show significant differences between cohabitation and

[3] Linda J. Waite and Kara Joyner, "Emotional and Physical Satisfaction with Sex in Married, Cohabiting, and Dating Sexual Unions: Do Men and Women Differ?", in *Sex, Love, and Health in America*, ed. Edward O. Laumann and Robert T. Michaels (Chicago: University of Chicago Press, 2001), 239–69; Judith Treas and Deirdre Giesen, "Sexual Infidelity among Married and Cohabiting Americans", *Journal of Marriage and the Family* 62 (2000): 48–60; Renate Forste and Koray Tanfer, "Sexual Exclusivity among Dating, Cohabiting, and Married Women", *Journal of Marriage and the Family* 58 (1996): 33–47; Paul R. Amato and Alan Booth, *A Generation at Risk* (Cambridge, Mass.: Harvard University Press, 1997), 258, table 4-2.

[4] See Stephen L. Nock, "A Comparison of Marriages and Cohabiting Relationships", *Journal of Family Issues* 16, no. 1 (1995): 53–76; Amy Mehraban Pienta, Mark D. Hayward, and Kristi Rahrig Jenkins, "Health Consequences of Marriage for the Retirement Years", *Journal of Family Issues* 21, no. 5 (2000): 559–86; Susan L. Brown, "The Effect of Union Type on Psychological Well-Being: Depression among Cohabitors versus Marrieds", *Journal of Health and Social Behavior* 41 (2000): 241–55; Susan L. Brown and Alan Booth, "Cohabitation versus Marriage: A Comparison of Relationship Quality", *Journal of Marriage and the Family* 58 (1996): 668–78.

marriage. As David Popenoe and Barbara Dafoe White-head point out, "Cohabitation typically does not bring the benefits—in physical health, wealth, and emotional wellbeing—that marriage does. In terms of these benefits, cohabitants in the United States more closely resemble singles than married couples. This is due, in part, to the fact that cohabitants tend not to be as committed as married couples, and they are more oriented toward their own personal autonomy and less to the wellbeing of their partner."[5] Married couples, as a group, have "greater sharing of economic and social resources" and a "better connection ... to the larger community".

These differences between cohabitation and marriage are often relevant not just for the couple but also for the children involved. Indeed, in the United States, four out of ten children spend part of their childhood being raised by cohabiting parents: "Approximately 24 percent of the nation's children are born to cohabiting couples, which means that more children are currently born to cohabiting couples than to single mothers. Another 20 percent or so of children spend time in a cohabiting household with an unrelated adult at some point later in their childhood, often after their parents' marriage breaks down."[6]

Marriage and cohabitation are not equally beneficial for the well-being of children. Child abuse is much more common among cohabiting households than among married

[5] David Popenoe and Barbara Dafoe Whitehead, *Should We Live Together? What Young Adults Need to Know about Cohabitation before Marriage; a Comprehensive Review of Recent Research*, 2nd ed. (New Brunswick, N.J.: National Marriage Project, Rutgers University, 2002), 5.

[6] W. Bradford Wilcox, *Why Marriage Matters: Thirty Conclusions from the Social Sciences*, 3rd ed. (New York: Broadway, 2011), 1.

households. Brad Wilcox notes, "When it comes to abuse, recent federal data indicate that children in cohabiting households are markedly more likely to be physically, sexually, and emotionally abused than children in both intact, married families and single-parent families."[7] The likelihood of sexual abuse is much higher in cohabiting families in which the man is not the biological father of the children in the house.

Children born to a cohabiting couple also have a much higher risk that their parents will break up than do children of a married couple. As Popenoe and Whitehead point out, "Fully three quarters of children born to cohabiting parents will see their parents split up before they reach age sixteen, whereas only about a third of children born to married parents face a similar fate."[8] Since cohabiting couples are more likely to break up than married couples, children end up at great risk for being raised by a single parent. Being raised by a single parent is itself linked to adverse outcomes for children, such as greater likelihood of arrest, greater likelihood of abuse of drugs and alcohol, and higher rates of dropping out of school.[9] Single-parent households are much more likely to live in poverty.[10]

In summary, the evidence is strong that cohabiting puts both the couple and any children involved at greater risk for adverse outcomes in comparison with marriage. Marriage, it turns out, is more than a piece of paper. Marriage makes a positive difference in a couple's mental and

[7] Ibid., 2.
[8] Popenoe and Whitehead, *Should We Live Together?*, 8.
[9] Stanton, *Why Marriage Matters*, chap. 4.
[10] Ibid., 117.

physical well-being, self-reported happiness, wealth, sexual satisfaction, and longevity. Marriage also makes a positive difference for children's mental and physical health, educational success, and likelihood of escaping poverty.

But there are still those who say that a wedding does not guarantee that a marriage will last, so why bother? They argue that the relationship will either survive or not, regardless of marriage.

This antimarriage argument is surely incorrect. After all, promises and signed contracts of all kinds are no guarantee that persons will fulfill their obligations, yet we still insist on them with respect to important matters in our lives, like cars, medical insurance, and jobs. Should we not bother with promises and contracts in these areas as well? After all, our employer either will or will not keep up his side of the bargain, so why bother making him promise? The reason is not hard to discern. Sometimes a promise, a contract, or a covenant helps ensure that someone fulfills an obligation. As the book *Influence: The Psychology of Persuasion* by Robert B. Cialdini points out, when people make a free, public, and active commitment to some cause, they are much more likely to follow through than if a free, public, and active commitment has not been made.[11] Many couples would not work as hard on their problems and would not make extra efforts to make the relationship work had they not promised to love each other in good times and in bad, in sickness and in health, till death do they part.

Other people may object, "Marriage changes nothing. Why does it matter?"

[11] Robert B. Cialdini, *Influence: The Psychology of Persuasion* (New York: HarperBusiness, 2006), 92.

I call this the "guy argument" because it is usually men who make it. But those who make this argument implicitly admit the truth about marriage even in their denials. If marriage changes nothing, then why are people (usually men) so reluctant to do it? Going to McDonald's rather than Burger King is no big deal. Watching one TV show rather than another is no big deal. If marriage is no big deal, then why not get married, if the other person wants to? I wish that those who hear from their romantic partners that marriage is no big deal would respond, "Great. If you feel that way, then it should be no big deal for you to let me have my way in such a trivial, insignificant matter. Let's set the marriage date for six months from this Saturday." I suspect that the men who say that marriage is no big deal would suddenly feel that it was a very big deal indeed.

Marriage *is* a big deal, for men and for women, because public promises are much different from private ones. It is one thing to pledge "eternal love" alone, at night, in the backseat of the car, during fleeting moments of passion. It is another thing entirely to say the same sorts of things in the light of day, before God and man, before a cloud of witnesses. Reneging on public vows carries with it a societal pressure that is absent from private promises. Society supports legally and socially married couples in a way that it does not support those who cohabit. Hence, married couples have a greater likelihood of making their love last forever.

Cohabitation and the High View of Marriage

The low view of marriage cannot justify cohabitation, but what about the high view of marriage? Is it true that living together prior to marriage decreases the likelihood of divorce? Does shacking up lead to less breaking up?

The empirical evidence gathered over decades is overwhelmingly clear that cohabitation does not reduce but rather increases the likelihood of divorce. As Stanton notes, "The overall association between premarital cohabitation and subsequent marital stability is striking. The dissolution rates of women who cohabit premaritally with their future spouse are, on average, nearly 80 percent higher than the rates of those who do not."[12] Zheng Wu, in his book *Cohabitation*, found that married couples who cohabit prior to their wedding may have double the likelihood of divorce when compared with those who do not.[13] Stanton points out:

> Sociologists at the Universities of Chicago and Michigan explain that the "expectation of a positive relationship between cohabitation and marital stability ... has been shattered in recent years by studies conducted in several Western countries, including Canada, Sweden, New Zealand, and the United States." Their data indicates that those who cohabit before marriage have substantially higher divorce rates than those who do not. In fact, the recorded differences range from 50 to 100 percent higher.[14]

Researchers discovered other striking findings as well about serial cohabitation. Serial cohabitation is a situation in which an individual lives with one person for a

[12] Stanton, *Why Marriage Matters*, 59.
[13] Zheng Wu, *Cohabitation* (New York: Oxford University Press, 2000), 149.
[14] Stanton, *Why Marriage Matters*, 57.

while and then, after a breakup, moves in with another person. Many people believe that serial cohabitation will help them to later have a happy, lasting marriage because they will be able to learn more about themselves and about the kind of potential spouse with whom they are most compatible. By a series of eliminations, this trial-and-error period will eventually lead to a more ideal marriage than would have otherwise been possible without a time of experimentation.

In fact, however, researchers found that living with a succession of different partners leads to an even greater likelihood of divorce than does living with one person prior to marriage.[15] This finding further calls into question the justification of cohabitation based on the high view of marriage. As Popenoe and Whitehead point out, "Contrary to popular wisdom, you do not learn to have better relationships from multiple failed cohabiting relationships. In fact, multiple cohabiting is a strong predictor of the failure of future relationships."[16]

Another surprise found in the research is that the longer a couple cohabits, the more likely they will divorce when they do marry.[17] Before I learned about this research, I had an acquaintance who had been living with his girlfriend for eight years. They then got married and were divorced within a year. I was completely shocked at this, thinking, "He must have known her well and had a solid relationship after eight years of living together. What could have possibly happened?" In fact, what happened to this

[15] Popenoe and Whitehead, *Should We Live Together?*, 15.
[16] Ibid.
[17] Ibid., 2.

acquaintance is not unusual. The research shows that "the longer you live together with a partner, the more likely it is that the low-commitment ethic of cohabitation will take hold, the opposite of what is required for a successful marriage."[18] No amount of cohabitation is helpful to a lasting marriage, but the longer that one cohabits, the worse it is for the long-term success of an eventual marriage.

Cohabitation and Divorce: Correlation, Causation, or Mutual Causality?

Scholars debate about how to understand the relationship between cohabitation and divorce. The two main rival views are the selection account and the causation account. The selection account holds that people who cohabit are already less likely to be committed to the institution of marriage, so when they enter it, they are less likely to persevere than are a married couple. Stanton explains this view as follows: "The first theory states that since cohabitors display greater attitudes of individuality, these attitudes ... are less likely to foster the kinds of behaviors necessary for a successful marriage: sacrifice, humility, flexibility, empathy, and the ability to delay gratification. In addition, the cohabiting partners commonly have a lowered view of and commitment to the institution of marriage."[19] In this view, cohabitation does not cause divorce, but people who are already more likely to divorce choose to cohabit. On the other hand, cohabitation itself could cause an increase in likelihood of divorce, as drunk driving causes an increased likelihood of accidents.

[18] Ibid., 15.
[19] Stanton, *Why Marriage Matters*, 5.

If it is true that cohabitation does not cause divorce but rather is only associated with divorce, then those who have the high view of marriage ought not to cohabit. Recall that the defense of cohabitation from the perspective of the high view of marriage is based on the belief that marriage is so important, and divorce so devastating, that you had better be as sure as possible that you have chosen the right person to marry. If it is true that people who choose to cohabit are less likely to have the behaviors and attitudes that facilitate flourishing marriages, then the willingness of a potential spouse to cohabit is some evidence that marriage is less likely to succeed with this person.

On the other hand, if cohabitation actually causes divorce by fostering and reinforcing behaviors and attitudes that undermine marital well-being, then of course those who wish to have a happy marriage should avoid cohabitation so as to increase the likelihood of lasting marriage. Many researchers support the causal explanation. As Popenoe and Whitehead suggest, "There is substantial empirical support for this position [that cohabitation is associated with divorce]. Yet, in most studies, even when this 'selection effect' is carefully controlled statistically, a negative effect of cohabitation on later marriage stability still remains. And no positive contribution of cohabitation to marriage has ever been found."[20]

I have found four different and compatible explanations of why cohabitation causes an increased likelihood of divorce. First, cohabitation causes divorce by reinforcing bad habits that undermine marriage. Whenever a person

---

[20]Popenoe and Whitehead, *Should We Live Together?*, 5.

moves into a new dwelling, especially with a new person, a new pattern of life and habits emerges. If a couple marries, then their habits of living are made in light of the status and role of the couple as husband and wife. If a couple are not married, then new habits are established in terms of the reality that the couple have not made the free, public, active, and often religious commitment of marital union. The habits are formed based on the couple's identities as unmarried single people. The research indicates that "cohabitants tend not to be as committed as married couples in their dedication to the continuation of the relationship and reluctance to terminate it, and they are more oriented toward their own personal autonomy. It is reasonable to speculate, based on these studies, that once this low-commitment, high-autonomy pattern of relating is learned, it becomes hard to unlearn."[21] Cohabitors live together with the expectations appropriate for non-married people. They build habits based on these expectations. Then when they wed, new expectations—those appropriate for husband and wife—come into conflict with the couple's established habits, creating contention and increasing the likelihood of divorce. In other words, when a cohabiting couple marry, although their habits of life do not change (they do not *begin* to live together), they do have new identities and a new relationship— husband and wife. A conflict arises between the established pattern of life that they have habituated themselves to and the new identities that they now have. This explanation also accounts for why the length of cohabitation matters

[21] Ibid.

in terms of the likelihood of divorce. The longer a couple cohabit, the more firmly the lower interdependence and commitment-averse behaviors and attitudes have been established.

A second explanation for why cohabitation causes divorce focuses on changed attitudes toward marriage.

> The results of several studies suggest that cohabitation may change partners' attitudes toward the institution of marriage, contributing to either making marriage less likely, or if marriage takes place, less successful. A 1997 longitudinal study conducted by demographers at Pennsylvania State University concluded, for example, "cohabitation increased young people's acceptance of divorce, but other independent living experiences did not." And "the more months of exposure to cohabitation that young people experienced, the less enthusiastic they were toward marriage and childbearing."[22]

We might rephrase this point by saying that cohabitation inclines a person toward contract unions and away from covenant marriage. The unconditional love of a covenant marriage makes it more likely both that a marriage will last as long as both spouses shall live and that this union will be happy and satisfying. By contrast, cohabitation makes couples more accepting of divorce, and by making them more accepting of divorce it makes them more likely both to actually divorce and to be unsatisfied with their marriage.[23]

The third explanation of why cohabitation causes divorce focuses on changes in attitudes of the cohabiting

---

[22] Ibid.
[23] Stanton, *Why Marriage Matters*, 68.

partners to one another. The character Samantha from *Sex in the City* once said, "Honey, before you buy the car, you take it for a test drive." When we consider the difference between those who have bought the car and those who merely take the car on an extended test drive, Samantha's adage reveals more than on its surface. As Daniel Gilbert writes in his book *Stumbling on Happiness*, "Committed owners attend to a car's virtues and overlook its flaws, thus cooking the facts to produce a banquet of satisfaction, but the [test drive] buyer for whom escape is still possible (and whose defenses are not yet triggered) is likely to evaluate the new car more critically, paying special attention to its imperfections as [he] tries to decide whether to keep it."[24] If car buying and test driving are indeed analogous to marriage and cohabitation, we would find (to paraphrase Gilbert) that married persons attend to each other's virtues and overlook each other's flaws, thus viewing the reality in such a way as to produce a banquet of satisfaction. The cohabiting partner, by contrast, for whom escape is still possible (and whose defenses are not yet triggered) is likely to evaluate his live-in lover more critically, paying special attention to her imperfections as he tries to decide whether to keep her—not exactly a recipe for love, let alone unconditional love. In the words of one woman who cohabited, "I felt like I was on this multiyear, never-ending audition to be his wife."[25]

A fourth account of why couples who cohabit tend to have a higher divorce rate is that cohabitors tend to "slide"

[24] Daniel Gilbert, *Stumbling on Happiness* (New York: Vintage, 2007), 204.
[25] Meg Jay, "The Downside of Cohabiting before Marriage", *New York Times*, April 15, 2012, SR4.

into marriage rather than decide to marry as those who do not live together prior to marriage.[26] Meg Jay explains the "sliding, not deciding" phenomenon as follows:

> Women are more likely to view cohabitation as a step toward marriage, while men are more likely to see it as a way to test a relationship or postpone commitment, and this gender asymmetry is associated with negative interactions and lower levels of commitment even after the relationship progresses to marriage. One thing men and women do agree on, however, is that their standards for a live-in partner are lower than they are for a spouse. Sliding into cohabitation wouldn't be a problem if sliding out were as easy. But it isn't. Too often, young adults enter into what they imagine will be low-cost, low-risk living situations only to find themselves unable to get out months, even years, later. It's like signing up for a credit card with 0 percent interest. At the end of 12 months when the interest goes up to 23 percent you feel stuck because your balance is too high to pay off. In fact, cohabitation can be exactly like that. In behavioral economics, it's called consumer lock-in. Lock-in is the decreased likelihood to search for, or change to, another option once an investment in something has been made. The greater the setup costs, the less likely we are to move to another, even better, situation, especially when faced with switching costs, or the time, money and effort it requires to make a change. Cohabitation is loaded with setup and switching costs. Living together can be fun and economical, and the setup costs are subtly woven in. After years of living among roommates' junky old stuff, couples

---

[26] See Scott M. Stanley, Galena Kline Rhoades, and Howard J. Markman, "Sliding versus Deciding: Inertia and the Premarital Cohabitation Effect", *Family Relations* 55 (October 2006), 499–509.

happily split the rent on a nice one-bedroom apartment. They share wireless and pets and enjoy shopping for new furniture together. Later, these setup and switching costs have an impact on how likely they are to leave.[27]

In other words, couples have lower standards for whom they would choose to live with in comparison to whom they would choose to marry. As the cohabiting relationship continues, both parties become more and more invested in time, energy, and various connections (perhaps even a baby), which push them, as they get older, toward marriage. Eventually, just as they slid into cohabitation, they slide into marriage, even though the relationship and the spouse are not what they would have chosen had they not cohabited.

It could turn out that both selection of spouse and causality are at play in the linkage between cohabitation and divorce. Mutual causality, or two-way causality, is illustrated by the following examples. Happy people tend to make more friends, and in making more friends they become happier still. Likewise, sick people tend to exercise less often than healthy people, and by neglecting exercise the ailing people become even more unhealthy. Similarly, cohabitation may be associated with divorce because commitment-phobic people more inclined to divorce are also more likely to choose to cohabit, and at the same time cohabitation may cause divorce by reinforcing attitudes and habits that undermine marriages.

Even if there were no association between cohabitation and divorce, couples should avoid cohabitation prior to

[27] Jay, "Downside of Cohabiting", SR4.

marriage for the sake of the later flourishing of a marriage. Even aside from the risk of divorce, couples who had cohabited had more problems in marriage than couples who did not cohabit:

> Research done at the University of California, Los Angeles, and published in the *Journal of Personality Assessment*, looked at the difference in "problem areas" for married couples who did and did not cohabit prior to marriage. Of some twenty problem areas, drunkenness, adultery and drug abuse (in that order) were the top three problems that distinguished married couples who lived together before marriage from couples who did not cohabit prior to marriage. The authors Michael Newcomb and P. M. Bentler explain: "In regard to problem areas, it was found that cohabitors experienced significantly more difficulty in their marriages with adultery, alcohol, drugs, and independence than couples who had not cohabited."[28]

In addition, it was also discovered that couples who cohabited prior to their marriage reported that they were less happy and satisfied in their marriage than those who did not. Stanton notes:

> Couples who lived together before marriage also "separated more often, sought counseling more often, and regarded marriage as a less important part of their life" than those who did not live together before marriage. Alan Booth and David Johnson, working from the University of Nebraska, studied 2,033 married couples in a national representative sample and found that the data does "not support the model that cohabitation

[28] Stanton, *Why Marriage Matters*, 60.

improves marital quality and reduces marital instability because it serves as a training period for marriage or improves mate selection." They concluded this because "cohabitation is not related to marital happiness, but it is related to lower levels of marital interaction, higher levels of marital disagreement, and marital instability." Further, they said, "On the basis of the analysis presented so far, we must reject the argument that cohabitation provides superior training for marriage or improves mate selection."[29]

Those who wish to increase the likelihood of happy marriage would do well to avoid cohabitation.

Gender Equality and Rationalizations for Cohabitation

Finally, let us consider the question, does cohabitation affect men and women equally? Most cohabitors want to get married at some point in their lives. It turns out that men and women typically look for different qualities in potential spouses. David Bess, in his book *The Evolution of Desire*, points out that around the world, men value youth and beauty in a spouse more than do women.[30] To anyone familiar with the human experience, the fact that men prefer young and beautiful women in preference to old and ugly ones is hardly surprising. Bess is not claiming that women do not care about having a handsome husband but rather that when seeking a spouse, women value the youth and looks of a potential husband less than men value

---

[29] Ibid., 58.
[30] David Bess, *The Evolution of Desire: Strategies of Human Making* (New York: Basic Books, 1994), 25.

the youth and beauty of a potential wife. Bess also found that worldwide, women value good financial prospects in a marriage partner more than do men.[31] Again, he is not saying that men would not prefer a rich wife to a poor one but rather that women tend to care more about good financial prospects when looking for a spouse than do men. Bess' findings explain why the very rich older man with a young and beautiful wife is a relatively common pairing and why the average age of first marriage for women is in every society younger than the average age of first marriage for men.

How are these observations relevant to cohabitation? Let us consider a concrete example. If a man and a woman decide to live together when they are both twenty-five years old, what is likely to happen? If they are like most cohabiting couples, several years later they will not be married. "After 5 to 7 years, 39% of all cohabiting couples have broken their relationship, 40% have married (although the marriage might not have lasted), and only 21% are still cohabiting."[32] So now the man and the woman are both unmarried at thirty-two. Characteristically, the man now has *more* of what most women want in a spouse. He has more earning power, and he has advanced his career. He is more mature, stable, and capable of supporting a family. By contrast, the woman is in a different situation. Characteristically, the woman now has *less* of what most men want in a spouse, namely, youth and beauty. So relative to when they began to live together, the man has gained and the woman has lost. Mark Regnerus and Jeremy Uecker, in their book *Premarital Sex in America: How Young Americans*

---

[31] Ibid., 50.
[32] Popenoe and Whitehead, *Should We Live Together?*, 2.

Meet, Mate, and Think about Marrying, put the point as follows: "For women, age is a debit in sexual economics theory, gradually drawing down physical attractiveness and perceived fertility. For men, age is a credit, heightening their access to resources and making them more attractive to women. It's also a more reliable predictor of maturity. Young women are generally more interested in settling into a stable and secure relationship than men of the same age are, and women often presume that older men have already acquired some relationship skills."[33] After a live-in relationship, the cohabiting man is in a stronger position vis-à-vis potential marriage mates than before the cohabitation; the cohabiting woman is in a weaker position. The man has become more valuable in the marriage market; the woman has become less "marketable". We can generalize by saying that women have more to lose in cohabitation, particularly in long-term cohabitation, than do men.

What drives cohabitation, besides low and high views of marriage? Many factors can be involved, but I will address a few of the most common. In some cases, the couple are very much in love and plans eventually to marry but consider themselves too young to get married.

In what sense are the couple "too young"? Clearly, they are old enough to consider moving in together, so why would they also not be old enough to marry? What may be behind the idea that the couple are too young is the view that marriages of the young tend to break up more than marriages of the more mature. This view is true, if

[33] Mark Regnerus and Jeremy Uecker, *Premarital Sex in America: How Young Americans Meet, Mate, and Think about Marrying* (New York: Oxford University Press, 2011), 78.

by "young" is meant teenage couples. The likelihood of divorce for eighteen- and nineteen-year-olds is very high indeed. However, the statistics change rapidly when a couple are in their twenties. Regnerus and Uecker point out, "The most *significant* leap in avoiding divorce occurs by simply waiting to marry until you're 21. The differences in success between, say, marrying at 23 and marrying at 28 are just not as substantial as many emerging adults believe them to be. And among men, there are really no notable differences to speak of."[34] Indeed, as we have seen, if a couple really want to lower the likelihood of divorce, they ought to avoid cohabitation. A relatively early marriage (again, not in the teen years, but not too long after that), rather than contributing to divorce, is linked to *higher* rates of marital happiness.

Regnerus and Uecker report:

> Respondents who marry between ages 22 and 25 express greater marital satisfaction than do those who marry later than that. In other words, the conventional wisdom about the obvious benefits (to marital happiness) of delayed marriage overreaches. Why it is that people who wait into their late 20s and 30s may experience less marital success rather than more is not entirely clear—and the finding itself is subject to debate. But it may be a byproduct of their greater rates of cohabitation.[35]

This same conclusion was reached by other scholars:

> One recent study by Norval Glenn and Jeremy Uecker examined five different large data sets and concluded,

[34] Ibid., 180. Emphasis in original.
[35] Ibid., 181.

"the greatest indicated likelihood of being in an intact marriage of the highest quality is among those who married at ages 22–25." The research also suggests that couples who marry in their twenties have more frequent sex and are more likely to hold a common faith and share common memories and family traditions—all factors that foster high marital quality. Our own analysis of the 2003–2004 National Fatherhood Initiative's marriage survey suggests that women are most likely to be happy when they marry in their mid-twenties.[36]

So while being too young is a reasonable consideration for a teenage couple not to marry, the empirical evidence suggests that a couple in their midtwenties—the age at which a couple are most likely to cohabit—who marry do not substantially increase their likelihood of divorcing. Indeed, a couple marrying in their early twenties will likely be better off in terms of marital happiness than a couple who wait until their late twenties or later.

Another reason sometimes given for choosing cohabitation over marriage is that the couple cannot afford to get married. This reason is surely misstated, since a marriage license is inexpensive and the state of being married is free. What is really at issue is a wedding. It is certainly true in many cases that a couple cannot afford a lavish wedding. But enjoying a grand wedding is, presumably, much less important than enjoying a lasting, happy marriage. The fantasy wedding should not be purchased at the risk of

[36] Kay Hymowitz, Jason S. Carroll, W. Bradford Wilcox, and Kelleen Kaye, *Knot Yet: The Benefits and Costs of Delayed Marriage in America; What Does the Rising Marriage Age Mean for Twentysomething Women, Men, and Families?* ([Charlottesville, Va.]: National Marriage Project at the University of Virginia, 2013), 20.

a nightmare marriage. What good is imitating a celebrity wedding if shortly afterward one imitates the celebrity divorce? It is much better to have a modest, simple wedding than to undermine the future happiness of husband, wife, and possible children through cohabitation.

Even considered purely in financial terms, to be married has financial advantages over cohabitation:

> Children are less likely to thrive in cohabiting households, compared to intact, married families. On many social, educational, and psychological outcomes, children in cohabiting house-holds do significantly worse than children in intact, married families, and about as poorly as children living in single-parent families. And when it comes to abuse, recent federal data indicate that children in cohabiting households are markedly more likely to be physically, sexually, and emotionally abused than children in both intact, married families and single-parent families.[37]

Regnerus and Uecker note that another reason given for choosing cohabitation over marriage is so that you can "be your own person". Many want to "find out" who they are. Being unmarried is seen in this view as the key to growth and maturity.

But of course, you can be your own person in marriage. If being your own person includes experiencing the happiness derived from loving God and other people, that can be found in abundance in marriage, insofar as one has made a concrete and specific vow to love a particular person and the children resulting from this union. As for

---

[37]Popenoe and Whitehead, *Should We Live Together?*, 9.

finding out who you are, self-knowledge is an ongoing process that does not conclude at the wedding ceremony. "Know thyself" is an adage that continues all through life. Knowing yourself is characteristically enhanced by conversation with someone who may know you better in some ways than you know yourself. In many cases, this person is a spouse. Marriage does not destroy individuality or inhibit self-knowledge any more than cohabitation or remaining unattached do. Indeed, in many cases, the reverse is true. Marriage, precisely because of its demanding nature—especially when children are involved—is an opportunity for spouses to become more virtuous and thereby find greater happiness.

Other people choose cohabitation over marriage because of the influence of their parents, note Regnerus and Uecker. Parents sometimes labor under misunderstandings about marriage and cohabitation. They believe myths, such as that cohabitation reduces the likelihood of divorce or that getting married at twenty-four will increase the likelihood of divorce. Parents who understand the reality of cohabitation would not encourage living together, particularly for their daughters, who are placed at greater disadvantage than men in cohabitation.

Regnerus and Uecker also speak of the "travel narrative" as a rationale for not marrying and choosing cohabitation instead. But of course, people *can* travel when they are married. It is not as if right after the wedding ceremony, a government official comes by and rips up the passports of the bride and groom. Married people can and do travel, together and sometimes alone. In the space of two years, I, as a married man, traveled from Los Angeles to Washington, D.C.; Minneapolis; Seattle; Princeton; Notre Dame; England; Israel; and South Africa. Marriage and travel are not mutually exclusive.

A final reason noted by Regnerus and Uecker for choosing cohabitation over marriage is that the couple believe that it is too soon to have children. However, getting married does not necessitate having children immediately. It is possible to be married without children, and as we have seen, cohabitation very often does involve children.

This chapter has examined cohabitation but has left one important argument against cohabitation entirely unexamined. Cohabitation, of its very nature, is something that an altruist should never do because it involves a kind of act that is intrinsically opposed to love. Love (agape) seeks to do good for the other for the other's sake. Love is therefore opposed to every action that intentionally harms other people—murder, theft, assault. Love is also opposed to actions that do not *intentionally* harm others, but needlessly endanger and unjustifiably risk others' well-being—such as driving drunk or shooting a gun in the air over a crowed city. People who are just do not risk the well-being of other people. Love also opposes actions that are untruthful, show a lack of integrity, and misrepresent the truth.

The next chapter provides an additional argument against cohabitation. It argues that cohabitation intrinsically involves a practice that friends of virtue do not choose. The next chapter takes up the issue of sex outside of marriage.

The Fifth Big Myth

"Premarital Sex Is No Big Deal"

The Reality: Marital acts without marital vows
characteristically endanger others and always
misrepresent the truth about the relationship.

In this chapter, I provide two arguments why sex outside of marriage is contrary to the happiness that is found in loving God and loving neighbor. One of the arguments appeals to consequences, and the other does not. Before exploring the ethics of sex outside of marriage, it may be helpful to situate the discussion by examining some myths about premarital sex that can distort clear thinking about the issue.

Myths about Premarital Sex

Mark Regnerus and Jeremy Uecker's book *Premarital Sex in America: How Young Americans Meet, Mate, and Think about Marrying* suggests that "pluralistic ignorance" informs many of the decisions that young adults, eighteen to twenty-three, make about sex. Unwritten scripts often shape behavior, and misinformation about the social world distorts the thinking of many people in this age group.

The first myth that Regnerus and Uecker dispel about premarital sex is "Everyone is doing it." In fact, everyone is *not* doing it. About a quarter of all college students have never had sex even once; a substantial percentage have had sex once before but regret it. Most college students are not in an ongoing sexual relationship, nor are most college students frequently hooking up. The "Animal House" orgies of many movies are simply not an accurate depiction of the real-life experiences of the vast majority of college students. Although many people believe that college students have frequent random hookups—anything from kissing to sexual intercourse—Regnerus and Uecker point out that the average college student hooks up only one time per year and that "78 percent of women and 73 percent of men say they've regretted at least one hookup." [1]

Another premarital-sex myth dispelled by Regnerus and Uecker is "Only losers don't do it." In fact, college students are more likely to abstain than those who did not attend college or who dropped out of high school. College virgins "tend to be a self-confident and accomplished lot". [2] College students refraining from having sex do not do so for lack of opportunities (at least for women) or for lack of sexual desire, and they are not less physically attractive than their peers. [3] Among people who do have

---

[1] Mark Regnerus and Jeremy Uecker, *Premarital Sex in America: How Young Americans Meet, Mate, and Think about Marrying* (New York: Oxford University Press, 2011), 105–6.

[2] Ibid., 117.

[3] Ibid., 22.

premarital sex, college students and college graduates have fewer partners than those who never went to college.[4]

A final myth about premarital sex that is widely believed among young adults is "You need it to start a long-term relationship." In fact, the opposite is the case. Hookups seldom turn into actual romantic relationships. "[Just] 8 percent of both men and women reported having had sex first—before sensing romance—in at least one of their two most important relationships so far. That means that in key relationships, 92 percent of young adults said that nurturing romance and love came first, before sex. It is difficult to make it work the other way around."[5] Nor do "friends with benefits" arrangements typically lead to something more substantial. "Only 1 out of 10 actually blossom into a romantic relationship, due in part to another ironic finding—that the relationships themselves exhibit little passion. Since making passionate love is often about an emotional as well as a physical connect, perhaps it's not surprising that such associations spark but fail to generate real fire."[6] The reality is that early sex generally leads to an early end of the relationship, and the early introduction of sex tends to hinder rather than enhance other aspects of the relationship. Sex can become a central focus while the couple are together, so that they do not explore other aspects of each other and get to know each other as well as if sex were not involved. Rapid development of sex "can obscure many other aspects of the relationship that are equally critical, if not more, to its long-term success."[7]

[4] Ibid., 26.
[5] Ibid., 62.
[6] Ibid., 66.
[7] Ibid., 75–76.

The Ethics of Premarital Sex

Let us turn to the ethics of sex outside of marriage. We saw in the introduction how people who seek level three and level four happiness are the kind of people who try to foster the well-being of all human beings, both themselves and others. An altruist does not endanger his own well-being or the well-being of another without a serious reason.

Some people believe that if they are endangering only themselves or others who have consented, then this is not ethically wrong. The altruist should reject this view. After all, level three and level four happiness are about loving, serving, and helping *all* human beings—oneself included—so level three and four include proper self-respect, self-concern, and self-protection. To treat oneself as if one did not have intrinsic human dignity, or as if one were not a child of God made in the divine image (to use the language of those who seek level four happiness), is to undermine the universality of the demand of love. The duty to love applies to *all* human beings, without exception.

Sex outside of marriage endangers the well-being of those who have it. Aside from strictly monogamous couples—those who have had sex only with each other—those who sleep with people outside of marriage risk contracting or exposing others to sexually transmitted infections (STIs). How many new cases of STIs are diagnosed each year in the United States? When I ask students this question, they often answer half a million, or two million, or five million. The correct answer is nineteen million. If you add together the population of New York City, Los Angeles, Chicago, Houston, and Phoenix, you would still have more people contracting a sexually transmitted infection each year.

There are a wide variety of STIs—from the annoying, such as genital warts, to the deadly, such as HIV/AIDS. The most common STI is HPV, human papillomavirus, which can manifest as genital warts. HPV is the most common STI in the United States, with more than twenty million people infected, or 40 percent of all sexually active people. It is most harmful to females of high school and college age. HPV is associated with almost every case of cervical cancer, which kills more than four thousand women annually. The Centers for Disease Control and Prevention (CDC) reported to Congress that condoms do not prevent HPV, since it is transmitted by bodily contact and not simply by transmission of seminal fluid. Nor can vaccinations, such as Gardasil, fully protect against HPV. There are forty different strains of HPV; Gardasil protects against only four strains.

How likely are you to get an STI—or another STI? Let us say that the first time you have sex, you have sex with someone else who is also a virgin. Next, you have sex with someone who, like you, has had sex with only one other person. Your next partner, like you, has had sex with only two other people. What will your sexual exposure be in such a case?

Former U.S. surgeon general C. Everett Koop said, "When you have sex with someone, you are having sex with everyone they have had sex with for the last ten years, and everyone they and their partners have had sex with for the last ten years."[8]

Sex outside of marriage, in addition to exposing the participants to the physical dangers of STIs, also endangers

---

[8] C. Everett Koop, Address at the Institute of Politics, John F. Kennedy School of Government, Harvard University, February 10, 1987, http://profiles.nlm.nih.gov/ps/access/QQBCJN.ocr.

the partners' ability to have lasting love. Oxytocin, a hormone that causes human bonding, is released during sex and while nursing a baby. Studies have shown that as the number of an individual's sexual partners increases, the levels of oxytocin decrease, making it more difficult to bond emotionally and psychologically with later partners. According to a study by the CDC, women having no nonmarital sexual partners had an 80.47 percent chance at a stable marriage. By contrast, when a woman had just one nonmarital sexual partner, that chance dropped to 53.6 percent. If a woman had five sexual partners outside of marriage, she had only a 29.7 percent chance of a stable marriage. "The more lifetime partners women have had, the higher their depression-scale score and the likelihood of diagnosis, the more crying they report, the lower their life satisfaction, and the more likely it is that they are currently taking anti-depressants."[9]

Premarital sex is also linked to divorce. Population-based studies have linked premarital sexual behavior to increased risk of divorce.[10] As Regnerus and Uecker note, "The number of premarital partners is a good predictor of infidelity within marriage for both men and women."[11] If the

[9] Regnerus and Uecker, *Premarital Sex in America*, 143.

[10] T.B. Heaton, "Factors Contributing to Increasing Marital Stability in the United States", *Journal of Family Issues* 23(3) [2002]: 392–409; Joan R. Kahn and Kathryn A. London, "Premarital Sex and the Risk of Divorce", *Journal of Marriage and the Family*, 53 (1991): 845–55; E. Laumann, J.H. Gagnon, R.T. Michael, and S. Michaels, *The Social Organization of Sexuality: Sexual Practices in the United States* (Chicago: University of Chicago Press, 1994); Albrecht and J. Teachman, "Childhood Living Arrangements and the Risk of Premarital Intercourse", *Journal of Family Issues* 24 (2003): 867–94.

[11] Regnerus and Uecker, *Premarital Sex in America*, 191.

habit of switching sexual partners has been established, it is difficult to drop it after marriage.

The risks of course are not merely physical and not merely about future divorce. In William Sneck's *America* article "Premarital Divorce", he reflects on his own experience of living with students in dorms and speaks to a person who has been emotionally hurt by premarital sex.

> You have been married and are now divorced! Without benefit of clergy, you have been wed to your first (and subsequent) loves and now are suffering psychological effects like those from separation and divorce. As a late teen, you had plunged yourself into the deepest mutual experience of human intimacy possible, but without the societal supports and sanctions that accompany marriage. Now you are agonizing over the dismemberment of your "one flesh." Although not legally or ecclesiastically married, you have been emotionally wed, and now you suffer the pangs of divorce, without being able to name the trauma and garner the assistance of family and friends.[12]

Undoubtedly, many people have experienced firsthand or secondhand the emotional upheaval that feeling used or rejected sexually in a relationship can bring.

Premarital Pregnancy

All the above considerations about premarital sex can be regarded as being rooted in concern about the self. If I want to eliminate the possibility of contracting STIs, if

---

[12] William Sneck, "Premarital Divorce", *America* 177, no. 15 (1997): 27.

I want to reduce the likelihood of unstable future relationships and avoid divorce, I ought to abstain from sex
outside of marriage.

However, all these considerations can also be rooted in
concern for others. If I care about the health and future
relationship stability of my potential sexual partner, then I
should refrain from having sex for that person's sake. Anyone who finds happiness in love of neighbor and love of
God should avoid sex outside of marriage.

Does sex outside of marriage endanger the well-being
of anyone other than the couple? Indeed, it does. To have
premarital sex is to take a substantial risk that there will
be premarital pregnancy, and premarital pregnancy risks
the well-being—emotional and physical—of the child
conceived. Is unintended pregnancy common? Maggie
Gallagher points out, "By their late thirties, 60 percent of
American women had had at least one unintended pregnancy. Almost 4 in 10 women aged 40–44 had had at least
one unplanned birth."[13]

Obviously, without the use of contraception, pregnancy is highly likely. As Alexander Pruss notes, "Without
contraception, the likelihood of pregnancy resulting from
a single act of intercourse by a couple of reproductive age
is about 5% (that is, for women in their late 20s and early
30s).... In the case of unmarried women in long-term
committed relationships, assuming the likelihood of intercourse increases with desire, the actual conception probability will presumably be higher than 5% (in the work

[13] Maggie Gallagher, "Does Sex Make Babies? Marriage, Same-Sex Marriage and Legal Justifications for the Regulation of Intimacy in a Post-*Lawrence*
World", *Quinnipiac Law Review* 23 (2004): 455.

of Colombo, *et al.* the conception probability peaks at 42.9%)."[14]

Each act of sexual intercourse contributes to an increasing likelihood of pregnancy, as the likelihood of conception is cumulative over time. If a young couple have normal fertility, the likelihood of pregnancy is 20 percent after the first month of sex. After the second month, the likelihood of pregnancy rises to 36 percent; after the third month, to 49 percent; after the seventh month, to 79 percent; and after the twelfth month, to 93 percent. Clearly, pregnancy becomes overwhelmingly likely over time.

But what about contraception? Perhaps having sex without contraception risks a premarital pregnancy, but premarital sex with contraception would be acceptable. Of course there might be a tiny remote risk of pregnancy, even with the use of contraceptives, but there is also a tiny remote risk of dying from being hit by a falling asteroid or getting struck by lightning. Aren't negligible risks morally irrelevant?

The trouble with this argument is that pregnancy is not a tiny, negligible risk even when contraception is involved. Yes, contraception reduces the likelihood of pregnancy in comparison to when contraception is not used, but the risk remains substantial. Indeed, over time, pregnancy is the norm rather than the exception. Contraceptives often fail, leading to premarital pregnancy. Maggie Gallagher

[14]Alexander Pruss, *One Body: An Essay in Christian Sexual Ethics* (Notre Dame, Ind.: University of Notre Dame Press, 2013), 185. Pruss is citing A. Colombo., A. Mion, K. Passarin, and B. Scarpa, "Cervical Mucus Symptom and Daily Fecundability: First Results from a New Database", *Statistical Methods in Medical Research* 15 (2006): 161–80.

notes, "Almost half of all pregnancies were unintended in 1994. Some 53 percent of these occurred among women who were using contraceptives."[15] As Anthony Fisher points out, "Most abortions in Western countries occur among people who are already using contraceptives."[16] More than half of the women who obtain abortions were using some form of contraception during the month that they conceived (contraceptive failure, human or technological, takes place more than five hundred thousand times annually in the United States alone). James Trussel at Princeton University estimates that "there are 27,000 condom breaks in the United States each night". Trussel and Barbara Vaughan point out, "The risk of failure during typical use of reversible contraceptives [nonpermanent contraceptives, such as birth control pills or condoms] in the United States is not low—overall, 9% of women become pregnant *within one year of starting use.* The typical woman who uses reversible methods of contraception continuously from her 15th to her 45th birthday will experience 1.8 contraceptive failures."[17] Pruss notes, "The annual failure rate for the male condom was 17.8%, and for the pill it was 8.7%."[18]

Cumulative probability is also at work, making the risk of pregnancy for those using reversible forms of contraception

[15] Gallagher, "Does Sex Make Babies?", 455.

[16] Anthony Fisher, *Catholic Bioethics for a New Millennium* (Cambridge: Cambridge University Press, 2012), 180.

[17] James Trussell and Barbara Vaughan, "Contraceptive Failure, Method-Related Discontinuation, and Resumption of Use: Results from the 1995 National Survey of Family Growth", *Family Planning Perspectives* 31, no. 2 (March–April 1999): 71, (emphasis in original).

[18] Pruss, *One Body*, 226.

extremely high over time. "Within 3 months of the initiation of use of a reversible method of contraception, 4.2% of all women experienced a contraceptive failure.... At 6 months, 7.3% had experienced a failure, and by 12 months of use, 12.4% had experienced a contraceptive failure."[19] Even if a contraceptive is 99 percent effective, the likelihood of pregnancy becomes extremely high if that contraceptive is used for several years. John Ross points out, "That one percent risk taken monthly over ten years, accumulates to a *70% probability* that an unwanted pregnancy will occur during that period."[20] So, of four sexually active women on the pill from age eighteen to age twenty-eight, approximately three of them will get pregnant despite using contraception. It is no surprise that the average woman using reversible methods of contraception will have on average about two pregnancies over the course of her lifetime.[21]

Ironically, the use of contraceptives in some cases *increases* the likelihood of pregnancy over time by causing behavioral disinhibition. The use of contraception lowers the risk of pregnancy for any particular act of sexual intercourse; yet, when using contraception, many people will engage in sex with people that they would never have sex with were contraception not being used. Even if each sexual act is in itself less likely to result in pregnancy, there may be a higher overall likelihood of pregnancy because

[19] Kathryn Kost et al., "Estimates of Contraceptive Failure from the 2002 National Survey of Family Growth", *Contraception* 77 (2008): 14, as cited by Pruss, *One Body*, 185.
[20] John A. Ross, "Contraception: Short-Term vs. Long-Term Failure Rates", *Family Planning Perspectives* 21, no. 6 (1989): 275, (emphasis mine).
[21] Trussell and Vaughan, "Contraceptive Failure", 71.

there are more numerous sexual acts. Behavioral disinhibition explains why high rates of contraceptive use are linked with high rates of unwanted pregnancies. Contraception gives people the illusion that they are "safe" from pregnancy, so people choose to have sex with partners with whom they would never have sex were contraception not available.

A final way of thinking about the risk of pregnancy prior to marriage is by comparison with drunk driving. Drunk driving is wrong not because every single time someone drives drunk a death occurs but rather because drunk driving endangers the lives of others. In 2010 an estimated 10,228 people died as a result of drunk driving, one every forty-eight minutes.[22] About two-thirds of abortions each year in the United States are procured by women who have never been married; given 1.2 to 1.3 million abortions per year, there are almost a million unwanted pregnancies annually resulting from premarital sex, at least one every minute. Unlike freak accidents, such as being struck by lightning, unintended pregnancy outside of marriage is extremely common. How many of us know someone personally who became pregnant via sex outside of marriage? I am myself the result of such a pregnancy.

What is the immediate effect of a typical unplanned premarital pregnancy? Summarizing sociological research on women's experience, Paul Swope writes:

[22]U.S. Department of Transportation, National Highway Traffic Safety Administration (NHTSA), *Traffic Safety Facts 2010: Alcohol-Impaired Driving* (Washington, DC: NHTSA, 2012 [cited Sept. 28, 2012]). Available at URL: http://www-nrd.nhtsa.dot.gov/Pubs/811606.PDF.

> Unplanned motherhood ... represents a threat so great
> to modern women that it is perceived as equivalent
> to a "death of self." While the woman may rationally
> understand that this is not her own literal death, her
> emotional, subconscious reaction to carrying the child
> to term is that her life will be "over." ... The sudden
> intrusion of motherhood is perceived as a complete loss
> of control over their present and future selves. It shat-
> ters their sense of who they are and will become.[23]

The life of a woman with an unplanned premarital pregnancy is not of course literally over, but nevertheless many
women report that they feel as if life as they have known
it is coming to an end. According to Swope's study, many
women facing a pregnancy prior to marriage feel as if they
are faced with choices only among various evils.

If a pregnancy occurs outside of marriage, how can the
couple respond? There are only a few possible choices,
namely, abortion, single parenthood, cohabitation, adoption, and shotgun marriage. Each one of these responses,
to a lesser or greater degree, undermines the well-being of
the child conceived outside of marriage.

The most common response to a child conceived outside of marriage is abortion. In the United States, married women are the least likely to get an abortion. "Most
women getting abortions (83%) are unmarried; 67% have
never married, and 16% are separated, divorced, or widowed. Married women are significantly less likely than
unmarried women to resolve unintended pregnancies

---

[23] Paul Swope, "Abortion: A Failure to Communicate", *First Things* 82
(April 1988): 31–35, http://www.firstthings.com/article/2008/11/004-
abortion-a-failure-to-communicate-49.

through abortion."[24] At least some of the abortions procured by married women abort adulterous pregnancies, so the percentage of abortions due to sex outside of marriage is higher than 83 percent.

Almost everyone involved in the contentious abortion debate admits that abortion is not a positive choice for mother or offspring but a regrettable alternative. Even those in favor of legalized abortion often say it should be safe, legal, and rare. Abortion in the United States is, sadly, not at all rare. One-third of all pregnancies end in abortion, some 1.2 to 1.3 million pregnancies each year. "Research indicates that 83% of abortions are to unmarried women and another 16% are to women who are separated, divorced, or widowed. So, the vast majority of aborted pregnancies are brought about by sex outside marriage."[25]

This means that premarital sex ends in eight hundred thousand to 1.1 million abortions yearly, a cumulative total of more than tens of millions of abortions since *Roe v. Wade* legalized abortion in 1973. In my book *The Ethics of Abortion: Women's Rights, Human Life, and the Question of Justice*,[26] I argue that abortion ends the life of a human being in utero and also point to evidence that abortion risks the psychological and physical well-being of the women. Therefore, abortion as a response to pregnancy

[24]Susan Dudley, "Women Who Have Abortions", National Abortion Federation, http://www.prochoice.org/pubs_research/publications/downloads/about_abortion/women_who_have_abortions.pdf.

[25] Rachel K. Jones, Jacqueline E. Darroch, Stanley K. Henshaw, "Patterns in the Socioeconomic Characteristics of Women Obtaining Abortions in 2000–2001", *Perspectives on Sexual and Reproductive Health* 34, no. 5 (2002): 226–35.

[26]Christopher Kaczor, *The Ethics of Abortion: Women's Rights, Human Life, and the Question of Justice* (New York: Routledge, 2010).

outside of marriage is radically incompatible with the identity of someone seeking level three and level four happiness. Recall that from a level three and a level four perspective, human beings have value even if they are vulnerable, dependent, and unwanted by others, so abortion cannot be justified on the basis that the unborn child is vulnerable, dependent, or unwanted. Abortion does not merely risk the well-being of the developing unborn human being but destroys it.

A second possible response to pregnancy outside of marriage is single parenthood. The mother alone, or less frequently the father alone, raises the child. Does single parenthood put children at risk for a disadvantaged life? The evidence is overwhelming and clear on this question. Although there are some fortunate exceptions, children of single parents generally have poorer school performance, lower rates of success in marriage, higher rates of drug and alcohol abuse, and higher rates of prison incarceration. They are also more likely to suffer physical and sexual abuse. In an *Atlantic Monthly* article, Barbara Dafoe Whitehead concludes her vast survey of social-science research as follows:

> Single-parent families are not able to do well economically.... In fact, most teeter on the economic brink, and many fall into poverty and welfare dependency. Growing up in a disrupted family does not enrich a child's life or expand the number of adults committed to the child's well-being. In fact, disrupted families threaten the psychological well-being of the children and diminish the investment of adult time and money in them. Family diversity in the form of increasing

numbers of single-parent and stepparent families does not strengthen the social fabric. It dramatically weakens and undermines society, placing new burdens on schools, courts, and prisons, and the welfare system. These new families are not an improvement on the nuclear family, nor are they even just as good, whether you look at outcomes for children or outcomes for society as a whole.[27]

Single parenthood risks putting both single parents and children at a disadvantage. There are certainly children of single parents who have been exceptions, but these exceptions do not alter the statistical probability that children of single parents are at greater risk of harm than children of married parents. Even risking such harm without good reason—especially risking the well-being of one's own child, for whom one has a special responsibility—is morally problematic. Because the overwhelming empirical evidence is that single parenthood risks the well-being of children, it is a choice incompatible with level three and four happiness.

A third possible response to pregnancy outside of marriage is cohabitation. The previous chapter noted the serious problems of this choice for the well-being both of the couple—including an increase in the likelihood of future divorce—and of the children. Children raised in a cohabiting environment are more likely to suffer physical and sexual abuse and more likely to see their parents break up. Cohabitation, like single parenthood, endangers the well-being of the child.

[27]Barbara Dafoe Whitehead, "Dan Quayle Was Right", *Atlantic Monthly*, April 1993, http://www.theatlantic.com/politics/family/danquayl.htm.

A fourth option when a couple are faced with a premarital pregnancy is adoption. This is often the best response, all things considered. I have greatly benefited by being adopted myself, and so I know from firsthand experience how adoption can make the best out of a tremendously difficult situation. Yet even if adoption is the best choice, premarital sex has still created a gravely imperfect situation. As those involved can attest, adoptions often cause intense emotional upheaval for birth parents, adoptive parents, and adopted children. Particularly from the perspective of the expecting birth mother, this choice seems extremely unattractive. Nevertheless, in many cases this choice is the one that is in a child's best interest. Summarizing the sociological research, Swope notes:

> Adoption, unfortunately, is seen as the most "evil" of [possible responses to unplanned pregnancy], as it is perceived as a kind of double death. First, the death of self, as the woman would have to accept motherhood by carrying the baby to term. Further, not only would the woman be a mother, but she would perceive herself as a bad mother, one who gave her own child away to strangers. The second death is the death of the child "through abandonment." A woman worries about the chance of her child being abused. She is further haunted by the uncertainty of the child's future, and about the possibility of the child returning to intrude on her own life many years later. Basically, a woman desperately wants a sense of resolution to her crisis, and in her mind, adoption leaves the situation the most unresolved, with uncertainty and guilt as far as she can see for both herself and her child. As much as we might like to see the slogan "Adoption, Not Abortion"

embraced by women, this study suggests that in pitting adoption against abortion, adoption will be the hands-down loser.[28]

Adoption is a loving, indeed a heroic, choice, but it is also a difficult one that many women find themselves unwilling to make. I will always be grateful to my own birth mother for the choice she made, but some women lack the heroism that my birth mother showed. Some birth fathers as well sense a feeling of great loss at placing a child for adoption. Sadly, some biological fathers push for abortion as a means to avoid parental responsibility and a permanent connection with the birth mother. From the perspective of the adopted child, while some children are perfectly adjusted and at ease with their adoptive parents, others feel deeply unsettled. Of course, this is vastly better than having one's life destroyed in utero, but it is still far from ideal.

The final option in the case of a premarital pregnancy is marriage. Shotgun marriages can and have worked. However, generally it is not a good idea to make such an important, life-changing decision under the pressure of dealing with an unplanned pregnancy. Many couples would have never married had they not gotten pregnant beforehand; other couples would have wisely chosen to wait until later. Couples who married under these circumstances may be forever haunted by the idea that were it not for the child's conception, there would have never been a wedding. Thus, premarital pregnancy can cast a shadow of doubt on the intentions of the spouses in entering marriage, which can itself undermine the marriage. Also, it

[28] Swope, "Abortion", 31–35.

takes great courage to make a commitment under those conditions. Many couples lack that courage and so choose abortion.

In sum, each of the responses to pregnancy outside of marriage endangers the well-being of the child to a greater or lesser degree. Since it is wrong to endanger the well-being of another without a serious reason, and since sex outside of marriage endangers the well-being of another—namely, the child conceived outside of marriage—without a serious reason, the altruist and the altruist of faith avoid sex outside of marriage.

Sexual Compatibility

Some might suggest that premarital sex is justified because it is necessary to make sure that a couple are "sexually compatible" prior to making the commitment of marriage. After all, it would be terrible to get married and then realize that sex with this particular person was disappointing, unsatisfying, or otherwise problematic.

Note, however, that this rationale is in play only in a scenario in which the possible sexual partner is seriously considered as a potential spouse. Casual sex or sex with someone who is not a serious marriage possibility could not be justified by the desire to find out if there was "sexual compatibility" suitable for marriage.

What is "sexual compatibility"? We can distinguish three separate meanings. First, it might mean that couples feel sexual attraction and erotic longing for one another. But clearly the act of sexual intercourse is not necessary to determine if a spark of attraction exists between two people. Often a glance or a short conversation can determine whether a couple find each other sexually alluring. Indeed, the desire to have sexual intercourse is characteristically already present prior to the choice to have sex. If potential spouses do not find one another attractive, sexual intercourse is not needed to find out whether one will desire to have sexual intercourse with the other.

Sexual compatibility in a second sense might be understood in terms of simple biological mechanics. Physiologically speaking, is there compatibility, a fit between the couple? If a gigantic man were to marry a diminutive woman, there might be some question. But sexual intercourse would not be needed to determine sexual compatibility in this second sense either, though a visit to a physician might be. Presumably, couples do not worry about "fit" in this biological sense. In the extremely rare case in which this actually becomes an issue, it is possible to undergo medical treatment for what physicians call vaginismus to resolve the issue of sexual compatibility in a biological sense.

A third sense of sexual compatibility is that the couple will have enjoyable sex, good sex. Justifying premarital sex on this basis also fails, since good (or bad) premarital sex does not ensure good (or bad) marital sex. The nature and quality of the relationship in general informs the sexual relationship as well. A kiss in love may be better than sex with no love. But if the relationship in general informs the sexual relationship, then sex before marriage would not necessarily be the same as sex after marriage, since the relationship before marriage is not the same as the relationship after marriage. So the sex before marriage might be great (due to the thrill of the "forbidden"), while the sex after marriage might be routine. Or the sex before marriage might be less enjoyable (due to fear of pregnancy, and a lack of security and commitment inhibiting a full gift of self), while the sex within marriage might be much more satisfying. For example, a friend of mine told me that prior to his marriage, sex with his future wife was amazing, a "swinging from the chandeliers" kind of sex. After the wedding, the sexual relationship was more akin to a desert with a few tumbleweeds blowing by in the cold wind. However, researchers consistently find that most couples experience the opposite effect: sex prior to marriage may be harried, anxious, and unsatisfying, but in the depth of the marital relationship the couple find their way to a satisfying sex life. Because premarital sex is not determinative of sexual enjoyment once the couple are married, sexual compatibility in this third sense does not provide a serious reason for sex outside of marriage.

Indeed, although some couples think that they have to determine whether they are sexually compatible before making a commitment, a study by researchers Dean M. Busby, Jason S. Carroll, and Brian J. Willoughby found that sexual restraint rather than sexual exploration of compatibility was linked with positive relationships. "It is clear that the longer a couple waited to become sexually involved the better their sexual quality, relationship communication, relationship satisfaction, and perceived relationship stability was in marriage, even when controlling for a variety of other variables such as the number of sexual partners, education, religiosity, and relationship length."[29]

---

[29] Dean M. Busby, Jason S. Carroll, and Brian J. Willoughby, "Compatibility or Restraint? The Effects of Sexual Timing on Marriage Relationships", *Journal of Family Psychology* 24, no. 6 (2010): 772.

Those seeking higher-quality relationships would be well served by delaying sexual activity until marriage.

One difficulty in understanding why premarital sex is wrong arises from understanding "All premarital sex is morally problematic" as "All premarital sex is equally problematic." As with killing, or any other sort of moral act, circumstances matter. Intercourse with a fiancé is not as bad as intercourse with a stranger. The difference depends upon the degree to which pregnancy is risked and the degree to which the couple are prepared to take responsibility for their actions. The greater the likelihood of pregnancy and the less prepared a couple are to be responsible parents, the more dubious their actions. Clearly, two actions can both be intrinsically evil, always wrong to do, and yet not equally wrong. Following Saint Augustine, one might argue that it is always wrong to lie and yet still suggest that not all lies are equally bad. It is worse to lie in court under oath than to lie in casual conversation. It is better to lie in defense of another's well-being than to lie for one's personal advantage. Similarly, it might be always wrong to steal and yet less wrong to steal from a rich person than from a poor person, and more serious to steal tons of money than just a little money. Sex outside of marriage is morally problematic in all cases, and yet one could still admit that casual sex is worse than sex before marriage in the context of marital engagement.

Truth and the Language of the Body

At the beginning of this chapter, I said I would offer two different arguments against premarital sex, one based on consequences and another that is not based on consequences. Let us turn now to this second argument.

Not all couples are fertile. What if one or both partners have been sterilized, and all possibility of offspring has been eliminated? And what if both partners know that they are free of STIs? If no children can possibly be conceived and no STIs can be contracted, then the arguments thus far given against premarital sex fail.

This objection must take into account the social nature of human beings. People are deeply influenced by the behaviors of others. Actions speak louder than words. The example of infertile couples engaging in premarital sex will influence willy-nilly the behavior of fertile couples, breaking down traditional prohibitions and social sanctions. To risk such breakdowns in the protection of potential children without a serious reason is morally irresponsible.

Let us take a case where pregnancy is impossible. It could be that the man and the woman are both sterile, or perhaps she has had a hysterectomy or is over sixty. Let us stipulate further that neither party has an STI and that no one will ever find out that they are having sex outside of marriage, and so social breakdown is not a factor. Even if all these conditions are met, a virtuous altruist would not have sex outside of marriage.

Virtuous people act and communicate with integrity and truth. Virtuous people avoid lying but rather communicate the truth. Lying to others undermines level three and level four happiness.

In truth, not all relationships are the same. A depth of intimacy and connection exists in some relationships but is missing in others. We rightly differentiate between the stranger, the acquaintance, the friend, the best friend, the family member, the fiancé, and the spouse. Because love responds to the reality of the beloved and to the relationship that exists with the beloved, the altruist takes such differences into account when choosing his actions.

When meeting someone, a virtuous person uses words that are fitting and true, corresponding with the occasion, such as "Nice to meet you." For friends, different words reflect the reality of the deeper relationship: "Hey, old buddy!" For family and very close friends, other words truthfully describe the reality of the relationship: "I love you, Mom." For a still more intimate relationship, that of an engaged couple, certain words are fittingly reserved. A virtuous man reserves the words "Will you marry me?" for his prospective fiancée alone, and a virtuous woman reserves the words "Yes, I will marry you" for her fiancé alone. (The roles of asker and the one asked are, of course, sometimes reversed.) For the most intimate relationship, that of husband and wife, a comprehensive union, distinctive words are fittingly and truthfully spoken only spouse to spouse: "I love you as my spouse for better or for worse, in sickness and in health, until death do us part."

Of course, it is possible to lie. We can use words in a way that distorts and misrepresents the reality of the relationship. When I was a freshman in high school, a senior on the soccer team gathered the underclassmen around and told us how to "score". He said, "If you want to have sex with a girl, it is really quite easy to get her to agree. Just take her out on a nice date, and when the time is right, look into her eyes and tell her, 'I love you.' And then she'll let you have sex with her." We were amazed.

Really? That is all you have to say? "Well," he confessed, "one time this didn't work. So I said to her, 'I *really* love you', and then we had sex." If a big lie does not do the trick, sometimes a bigger lie does.

Of course, he did not really love all these girls. He did not want a comprehensive union with them but just wanted to use their bodies for a while. He found a line—a lie, actually—that got him what he wanted. A virtuous person does not lie.

The words "I love you" mean something. Even before I started dating, I said to myself, "I'm not going to tell a girl that I love her until I want to marry her." So in high school and college, I did not tell any girlfriends that I loved them. In college, I started dating a young woman, and after a few months, she wondered why I had not said these words. I told her that I wanted these words really to mean something and that I wanted to say them only to someone with whom I wanted to spend the rest of my life. Then after a few more months, I signed a card to her with the words "I love you." Those words meant so much to her—and to me. I am happy to say that I have now been married to that woman for more than twenty years.

In a similar way, there can also be a fitting and truthful connection between our "body language" and our relationships. When we meet strangers, we shake their hand. When we meet our friends, we give them a hug. When we meet our family and close friends, we give them a kiss. A couple engaged to be married show the abundant affection that is fitting for their movement toward marriage, but that affection would be excessive and inappropriate for friends and family. A married couple—whose relationship is of the most intimate and the most comprehensive kind—engage in the marital act, the most intimate and the most comprehensive kind of language of the body.

It is of course possible to distort the connection between relationships and their corresponding language of the body. When we first meet someone, we could try to kiss and embrace the person like we would our mother or our best friend. An excessive display like this would be a kind of lie; this stranger is not our mother and is not our best friend. It would be possible to have sex with someone to whom we are not married, but this language of the body would be itself a lie, a misrepresentation of the reality of our relationship.

We do not have to tell the truth with our words or with our bodies. We could meet a total stranger and say, "I love you." We could call up our parents and say the marriage vows. We could pretend that we have a comprehensive union with someone who is not actually our spouse. Nothing would stop us.

But if we really did love someone, how would we communicate this love? If I said, "I love you" just to get someone to have sex with me, what would I say if I really did love someone? If I exchanged the marriage vows or engaged in the marital act with people I was not married to, how could I communicate this deepest kind of love and commitment if I finally found "the one"?

Alexander Pruss points out that sex outside of marriage is an act against love and against truth.

> [T]he couple is doing something that would be a consummation of fully committed romantic love,

something that joins the couple as one body, while deliberately leaving out the temporal dimension that commitment would have supplied. In choosing to leave out this temporal dimension, the couple opposes itself to romantic love while acting in a way that partially consummates it. By failing to be committed to each other, the two persons both unite as one body and leave it open to themselves to discontinue their union in the future, an option contrary to the meaning of organic union.... [T]heir actions are not grounded in truth, for in truth they *are* united as one flesh, whether they see this or not.[30]

A friend of virtue does not lie with words or with the body because liars act against level three and level four happiness. A friend of virtue does not act against love. Lying with words or the body undermines communication; it robs a person of the chance to express in a unique and meaningful way a depth of intimacy and commitment. This point still holds true in cases where premarital pregnancy is impossible or no other bad consequences can arise.

Is premarital sex the worst of injustices? Of course not. But justice, as well as charity, demands that we take quite seriously marital acts without marital vows.

In the next chapter, we will be considering the fruit of the marital act—children. How do children relate to erotic love? How do children relate to earthly happiness? How do they relate to our ultimate happiness, promised by Jesus in the life to come?

---

[30] Pruss, *One Body*, 176. Emphasis in original.

The Sixth Big Myth

"Children Are Irrelevant to Marriage"

*The Reality: Children contribute greatly
to the well-being of their parents.*

People still speak of the classic combination of "love, marriage, and baby carriage". Even the word "matrimony" (from the Latin *mater*, meaning mother, and *munus*, meaning mission, task, responsibility) shows the ancient linkage between marriage and children. In a literal sense, the state of matrimony is not merely a matter concerning the husband and wife alone but is ordered to the mission, task, and responsibility of motherhood (and fatherhood). The Second Vatican Council taught, "By their very nature, the institution of matrimony itself and conjugal love are ordained for the procreation and education of children.... Children are really the supreme gift of marriage and contribute very substantially to the welfare of their parents."[1] Yet the intimate connections between marriage, love, and procreation are not obvious

[1] Second Vatican Council, *Gaudium et Spes*, 48, 50, http://www.vatican.va /archive/hist_councils/ii_vatican_council/documents/vat-ii_const_19651207 _gaudium-et-spes_en.html.

in our culture. Although most married couples have children, the links between love, sexual activity, children, and the welfare of the parents are not always easy to see.[2] A large part of this dis-integration of marriage and parenthood comes from viewing children as an option or a hassle rather than a gift or a blessing.

Once I was giving a talk and asked a group of parents, "What do children give to parents?" The responses included "Gray hair", "Ulcers", and "Empty bank accounts". As a culture, we do not view children as something good for parents. Although good parents contribute substantially to the welfare of their children, we do not think that children characteristically return the favor. Perhaps on the family farm, children might contribute to the welfare of their parents by performing labor. Perhaps in other societies, children are needed to care for their parents in advanced old age. In our society, we tend to think that the benefit travels one way: from mother and father to offspring. The parents provide; the children receive. The parents give; the children get.

Yet the truth is richer than this simple picture. Children do give something to parents, and not just ties on Father's Day or flowers on Mother's Day. In an ideal situation, husband and wife share at least three identities. They are erotic lovers, best friends, and companions on the journey to heaven. It turns out that the procreation and

[2] The procreation and education of children should be understood together, in the sense that merely procreating children without providing sufficient care for their proper upbringing would be contrary to "responsible parenthood", the vocation of the married couple. In what follows, I speak for the most part of the procreation of children but always do so within the context of responsible parenthood, a matter for careful discernment by the couple.

education of children contribute greatly to all three facets of the spouses' relationship. Children help parents to realize the goal of erotic love—an exclusive and lasting union of lover and beloved. Children also help to strengthen the friendship between husband and wife, helping it to deepen. Finally, children help their parents on their journey toward heaven, making it easier for them to obey the commandments, which are prerequisites for entering into eternal life.

Procreation of Children and Marital Erotic Love

It might seem at first glance that the education and the procreation of children are an afterthought to the cozy arrangement of lover and beloved, an unwanted intrusion on the intimacy of the married couple. Admittedly, children do not contribute much, if anything, to erotic love if it is understood as mere animal magnetism, a physical attraction. Sexual attraction never extends to children, let alone one's own children, save among the most perverse. Although sexual attraction has a biological basis in signs of fertility,[3] procreation and sexual attraction are not necessarily related; indeed, sometimes they are inversely related. Bearing children sometimes renders a woman less physically attractive, at least according to the standards set by magazines, both those catering to the adolescent male as well as those aimed at young women. And if the procreation of children does not undermine the "zing" a couple once shared, there is a good chance that the education of

[3] David M. Bess, *The Evolution of Desire: Strategies of Human Mating*, rev. ed. (New York: Basic Books, 2003).

children will constrain the joys of the marital bed. The education of children, understood in its broadest sense of properly caring for them and raising them, very often stands in the way of enjoying bodily pleasures. Indeed, the cost and the attention required to raise a child properly channel energy and attention away from devotion to seeking bodily pleasures. Those who follow their pleasures and devote themselves wholeheartedly to bodily attractions—be they of food, drink, drugs, or sex—will find it difficult if not impossible to provide the good moral example to their children that is certainly an element of education in its proper and fullest sense. Physical attraction and the procreation and education of children stand in no small tension.

However, erotic love—as discussed in chapter 2—is much more than mere sexual attraction. In Genesis, for example, we find an account of erotic love that provides a close link between erotic longing and procreation. Adam finds no partner among the beasts, and his yearning for union is fulfilled only in Eve. This yearning and its completion—"This at last is bone of my bones and flesh of my flesh" (Gen 2:23)—take place before the fall. Likewise, the blessing "Be fruitful and multiply" occurs before the fall (Gen 1:28). The eros between Adam and Eve is part of the divine plan from the beginning and is in no way connected with punishment. Nothing satisfies the erotic longing of Adam until the creation of Eve. Following the fall, this relationship is tarnished. Adam, who failed to confront the threatening serpent with Eve, blames Eve for their situation and implicitly also blames God: "The woman whom you [God] gave to be with me, she gave me fruit of the tree"

(Gen 3:12).[4] Marital relations become *martial* for the first time. The first man fails to see his wife as a blessing from God. However, the erotic love of man and woman is a part of the original blessing of creation. This original blessing is damaged but not removed by original sin, a blessing linked from the beginning with a partial re-creation of the original unity of man and woman by means of the sexual act and the fruit of the sexual act, offspring.

In Plato's *Symposium*, the speech given by Aristophanes about the origins of erotic love differs radically from the account given in Genesis, yet in other ways it is surprisingly similar. As we explored in the second chapter, Aristophanes' story explains erotic love as arising from a punishment of Zeus that divided the original four-footed, four-handed human beings in half. The separation of the primordial humans, who appeared something like back-to-back conjoined twins, gave rise to the drive to reconnect, to reunify, to become one. Like in Genesis, the story of Aristophanes depicts erotic love as the drive toward unity of lover and beloved.

Sexual intercourse to some extent, and covenant marriage to an even greater extent, unifies a couple, but couples in love seek a still deeper unity. What would this deeper, more lasting, and exclusive personal unity look like?

It would look like a person. The desire to be one with the beloved is fulfilled through procreation. Every child of a couple creates a unique bond between them and them

---

[4] For a corrective to certain antifeminine interpretations of the fall that lay heavier blame on Eve than on Adam, see Scott Hahn, *A Father Who Keeps His Promises: God's Covenant Love in Scripture* (Ann Arbor, Mich.: Servant, 1998), chap. 3.

alone, a unity that not only preserves the individuality of the husband and the wife but manifests their individuality in a new way. Each child is an enduring expression of the unique union of the couple, this man and this woman. If eros is about exclusivity and eternity, a child bonds a couple to each other exclusively and for as long as the child shall live. In their offspring, a couple realize the dream offered by Hephaestus to be "rolled into one" and "welded together" and "never to be parted". So long as the child shall live, he is a living sign, a sacrament if you will, of the union of one man and one woman—a realization of the dream of eternal unity of lover and beloved. They become one flesh, and their one flesh union dwells among us.

The unity achieved by a married couple in procreation includes but also transcends a physical unity of various DNA strands. Each child creates in the parents a new unity, for the man and the woman together become parents to this child. A new and shared dimension is added to them both as they become, through each other, parents. She makes him a father; he makes her a mother. They share a lifelong unity as parents of their child. By begetting a child, they will forever be related to one another in a bond that remains in good times and in bad, in sickness and in health, so long as the child shall live. Children are an embodied manifestation of the vows of covenant marriage. In having children, the spouses share a lifelong and exclusive unity as parents of their child.

In addition to the embodied unity achieved in the child, and the familial unity of becoming parents to this child, characteristically a unity of affection and desire also arises between the parents ordered to the care of their child. Among happily married couples, this is most obvious as both mother and father busy themselves in direct and indirect collaboration in raising children. They coordinate plans and cooperate in the running of a home.

But even among those who are unhappily married or not married, characteristically there remains a unity of the parents in affection and desire for the well-being of their children. A divorced mother and father may positively hate one another, but they may also share an equal ferocity of parental love and desire for the well-being of their shared children. Indeed, the unity of love and affection for children is sometimes enough to overcome marital hatred, as when a divorced pair both act "on their best behavior" so as not to spoil a special event for a child or when a couple in crisis give yet another chance to their marriage so as to save the offspring from a broken home. Even turbulent marital strife characteristically does not shatter the unity of affection and desire achieved through procreation. The procreation and education of children realizes in its own way the deepest desires of eros for enduring unity, even after eros itself has long since departed.

United physically in the body of the child, united through mutual parenthood in the begetting of the child, united by affection in the care of the child, the procreation and education of offspring realizes, in a certain way, the dream of Aristophanes and the promise of Genesis—the two shall become one. The procreation and education of children should not be understood therefore in opposition to eros but rather as a fulfillment of the deepest aspirations of eros.

Erotic Love and Contraception

The point of contraception is to act against (contra) conception. Couples use contraception in order not to have a child. In having sex, their bodies are partially unified, but the goal of contraception is to make sure that part of the man (his sperm) does not unite with part of the woman (her ovum). How does this fit with erotic love? Erotic love is the drive toward unity; contraception seeks to block and prevent full unity. So the use of contraception, deliberately thwarting the procreative potentiality of a couple, contradicts the nature of erotic love.

Recall too that erotic love, as opposed to mere sexual attraction, involves a delight in and an appreciation of the whole person rather than a reduction of the person to simply what is pleasurable or useful. We all have different dimensions of ourselves, physical, social, mental, and spiritual. For healthy people of reproductive age, a part of our bodily well-being is our fertility. In contracepting, a choice is made not to accept an aspect of one's sexual partner (or of oneself). In using contraception, that part of the person that is the ability to become a father or a mother is intentionally rejected, at least for the time being. By contrast, erotic love delights in all aspects of the beloved— mind, soul, and body, including the fertility of the body.

If this analysis is correct, then erotic love and contraception work at cross purposes. Erotic love accepts and delights in the totality of the beloved and seeks unity with the beloved. Contraception involves a rejection, rather than an acceptance, of the whole person and seeks to thwart a full unity. Far from enhancing the erotic love of the couple, contraceptive acts are antierotic. Love and life, eros and procreation, belong together.

The Procreation and Education of Children and Marital Friendship

A good marriage involves much more than erotic love— it also includes friendship. Couples do not maintain the dizzying intoxication of the first flowering of erotic love forever. However, they can not only maintain but also deepen a marital friendship over time. Of all the time spouses spend together, only a small percentage is spent in sexual activities. Most of the time they are doing activities that they can and often do share with any mere friend— eating together, shopping, working, praying, exercising, chatting, cleaning, driving. In other words, in a good marriage, the couple are not merely erotic lovers but also friends, ideally best friends. What does having children do to this friendship? In chapter 1, we addressed what a friend really is, and we will now reconsider that subject.

People cannot be fully happy without friends. Who could really enjoy even the best things in life, if he were all alone? Aristotle concluded that real friends have mutual goodwill, common activity, and a shared emotional life. Each aspect of friendship is important. If we are kind to someone but the person is not kind in return, the two of us are not really friends. If we find out that someone that we thought was a friend has been backstabbing us, revealing our secrets, and stealing from us, we might say something like, "Well, I thought that Brett was my friend, but I now realize that he is not." If a person is kind to you but does not want to spend time with you, then he is not a true friend. Finally, real friends share in each other's joys and sorrows. When you get an A on a test, your friends are happy with you. When you lose your job, they are sad with you. In the roller-coaster ride of life, they share your triumphs and your tragedies, and you share their triumphs and tragedies as well.

How does all this relate to the friendship of a marital couple? As noted above, real friends have mutual goodwill for one another, and having children provides an additional motivation for the mother and father to have goodwill for each other. No marriage is an endless honeymoon. Every marriage encounters difficulties, and I think it is fair to say that most marriages encounter serious difficulties at some point. In times of trouble, one spouse or the other may say, "I've had enough. I give up. I want out." If the couple have children together, a weighty factor offers a counterbalance to these thoughts of ending the marriage and leaving altogether. When there are shared kids involved, leaving a spouse also involves leaving the children or leaving the children without their mother or their father. The love and affection parents have for children prompts many spouses in troubled times to reconsider plans to leave: "I cannot stand my spouse, but I do love the kids. I'll give it another chance." The presence of shared children provides a powerful incentive to both husband and wife to forgive each other, to make the best of an imperfect situation, and to be faithful to their vow of "for better or for worse, until death do us part".

Children also strengthen a marital friendship by giving rise to shared activity for the spouses. Meaningful, challenging activity is a prerequisite for happiness, as we explored in the first chapter, and the marital couple with children have a most meaningful task: to raise their children well. My wife and I, as the parents of seven children, share an abundance of meaningful, challenging joint activity. Indeed, each day is overflowing—wake up the kids and feed them breakfast; make sure their teeth and hair are brushed and drive them to school; oversee homework after school, drive them to dance lessons, pick them up from play practice, and talk to their basketball coach; get dinner ready and oversee chores; get them ready for bed, pray, and make sure they are getting to sleep. The typical married couple with children have abundant meaningful shared activity, the very stuff out of which friendship is made and strengthened. Raising children is the source of shared meaningful activity for the husband and wife.

Friendship also involves sharing an emotional life. The husband and wife share joys and hopes for their children, beginning prior to birth. The first words, the first steps, the first bike ride without training wheels, and the First Holy Communion can all bring tears of shared joy. The couple also share in the many moments of distress occasioned by their children: visits to the emergency room, academic or social trouble in school, and anxiety over the child's behavior. The parents rejoice together when their children do well; they suffer together when their children do poorly. They cry, laugh, worry, delight, and groan in union over the people that matter most in both of their lives—their children. My wife captured one such shared moment—when our eldest son left for college. She wrote:

I did not anticipate kissing his neck. I had thought only seldom, and very, very fleetingly, about the moment at all. In fact, I had spent more time trying *not* to think about the good-bye than I had spent considering how it would go. I am, you see, an expert suppressor. As a rule, I do not cry in public. In reality, I do not cry much at all. It makes me very uncomfortable. Partly, I am embarrassed by crying, but primarily, I am afraid that if I start, I will not be able to stop. Losing control of myself, physically or emotionally, has always been an enormous source of stress for me. Ironically, the simple fear of losing control causes me more stress than actually losing control. But such is the life of a neurotic. So saying good-bye to my beloved son as he left for college was not just something I was not looking forward to but was something I was dreading.

He left this morning. And so here I sit, at the computer, hoping that through writing about his departure, I can simply analyze my emotions instead of experiencing them. But his bedroom is right behind me ... and the door is ajar. When he lived here (yesterday) the door was not ajar. When he lived here, it was not only always closed, but it was always locked—the result of having six siblings. But today, from my writing desk, I can see the clothes he did not take, yesterday's socks, his football, and the various school papers and forms from senior year that no longer matter.

Except that all of those papers, all of those jumped-through hoops, earned him a scholarship and put him on a plane today. They put him a mile above the earth—above me. And I cannot get him back. I cannot get my six-pound, fourteen-ounce, slightly premature baby boy back. I cannot get the nervous toddler sitting stonily on Santa's lap back. I cannot get the imaginative, sword-wielding six-year-old back. I cannot get the basketball-obsessed twelve-year-old back. I cannot get the high-school football player back. And I have a headache from trying so hard not to cry.

This morning, at five thirty, it was time to say goodbye. His bags were packed. The Suburban was loaded. But he was suddenly hungry and asking for breakfast. Automatically, I warmed a hamburger—left over from his farewell dinner—and wrapped it in a paper towel, set in on a small plate, and held it, lamely, in my hand. We faced each other.

He felt sorry for me. I sensed it rather than saw it. I could not look at him. He muttered something about being home for Christmas. I said nothing. I wrapped my free arm around his neck, and then for one instinctive, primal moment, I nuzzled my lips into his neck, inhaled his scent, and kissed him softly.

I will probably never do that again. He will probably never let me. It was the most intimate moment we have shared since I stopped breast-feeding him—like a bookend set in place to secure his childhood.

Although I could not capture it in words, I shared her sense of deep loss. Thank God we have also shared moments of joy and exhilaration.

As mentioned earlier, Aristotle believed that a friendship of virtue would be more long lasting, rich, and satisfying than a friendship of utility or a friendship of pleasure. Because friends of virtue are loved for who they are rather than for merely what they give us (pleasure, utility), our love for them is more stable. Saint Thomas Aquinas wrote, "The greater a friendship is the more solid and long lasting will it be. Now there seems to be the greatest friendship between husband and wife, for they are united not only in the act of fleshly union, which produces a certain gentle association even among beasts, but also in the partnership of the whole range of domestic activity."[5] A couple could have a marital friendship of pleasure, a marital friendship of utility, or a marital friendship of virtue. Although children stand in the way of a marital friendship of pleasure or utility, offspring occasion a marital friendship of virtue.

People gain acquired virtue only through repeated performance of a good action. Just as no one can learn to play the piano in a day but rather can learn only through hours of practice, so too acquired virtues are gained only through countless repetitions. A just, temperate, courageous, and practically wise person must choose over and over again to do actions that are responsible, self-disciplined, brave, and shrewd. Couples who have children together have abundant opportunities to perform such good actions for their children and in doing so develop to a greater and greater degree the habits that are needed for true happiness.

The basic tasks that any good parent must do—such as taking care of the children's physical well-being, providing for their education, and correcting their behavior—also help the parent develop important virtues, such

[5] Thomas Aquinas, *Summa contra Gentiles*, trans. Vernon J. Bourke (Notre Dame, Ind.: University of Notre Dame Press, 1975), III, ch. 123, n. 6, p. 148.

as generosity, patience, responsibility, self-sacrifice, and compassion for the needs of others. The more developed a husband and wife become in these habits, the stronger their friendship of virtue becomes.

Empirical evidence also suggests that children strengthen, rather than undermine, marriages. Divorce is the death of a marriage, the exact opposite of both erotic love and marital friendship. Having children together is associated with a lesser likelihood of divorce. Mariah Wojdacz writes, "Having a baby seven months or more after marriage will give you a 24 percent decrease in chance of early divorce."[6] Psychologist David Bess made a similar finding: "According to a United Nations study of millions of people in forty-five societies, 39 percent of divorces occur when there are no children, 26 percent when there is only a single child, 19 percent where there are two, and less than 3 percent when there are four or more."[7]

A Way to Heaven: The Procreation and Education of Children

Some years ago, I began a talk by asking a group of parents, "How do children help their parents get to heaven?" Someone raised his hand and said, "You've got to go through hell before you can get to heaven." No doubt all seasoned parents can share a laugh in agreement—I know I can. We spend considerable worry, anxiety, and care on our children. But for Christians, the contribution of children does not simply include the difficulties but also

[6]Mariah Wojdacz, "Your Chances of Divorce May Be Much Lower than You Think", http://www.stateofourunions.org/2011/SOOU2011.php.
[7]David Bess, *The Evolution of Desire* (New York: Basic Books, 2003), 175.

transforms them. Indeed, children are a pathway for parents toward heaven.

How so? Jesus taught his followers, "If you would enter life, keep the commandments" (Mt 19:17). Having children aids parents in obeying a number of commandments, both of the Old Testament and the New Testament. One of the Ten Commandments is "Honor your father and your mother" (Ex 20:12). Raising children helps a person obey this commandment. It is only in taking on the daunting task of parenting that we can appreciate firsthand what our own parents did for us. Before I had kids of my own, I remember my haughty and hypercritical attitude toward my own parents. I remember thinking, "I'll do such a better job." Then, when my wife and I began to have kids, I was amazed at how demanding it is to raise children. I realized that given the limited resources of time, energy, and money, a parent cannot help but be imperfect, even with great effort. I came to be less and less critical of whatever perceived mistakes my parents had made with my sister and me. I became more and more grateful for all that my parents had done and continued to do for me because in trying to do similar things for my own kids I realized the enormous cost to my parents financially, physically, socially, and psychologically. The more I raise my own children, the easier it becomes to honor my own parents.

Children also help parents obey the first commandment. The very first of the Ten Commandments is "You shall have no other gods before me" (Ex 20:3). I used to think that this commandment was superfluous in modern times. Sure, in ancient times, people may have bowed down before golden calves or worshipped statues of bronze or forces of nature, but today, I was sure, almost no one violated this commandment. I was wrong. This is actually perhaps the most commonly violated commandment. Modern people tend not to worship statues or the powers of nature; they tend to worship themselves. They treat themselves as the most important thing in the universe. It is the common weakness of each person to make himself into a god, indeed the most important god. This tendency goes all the way back to the beginning. One interpretation of the story of the fall of Adam and Eve is that they also wanted to be gods, in control and the ultimate authority in the universe. "The serpent said to the woman, 'You will not die. For God knows that when you eat of it your eyes will be opened, and you will be like God, knowing good and evil'" (Gen 3:5). Trying to be gods or God is the original and perennial sin. Even aside from revelation, the atheistic philosopher Jean-Paul Sartre spoke of the universal human desire to be God. "To be man means to reach towards being God", wrote Sartre. "Or if you prefer, man fundamentally is the desire to be God."[8]

Young children know that they are not God. Someone else tells them when to get up, what to eat, what to do, and when to go to bed. Every detail of their young lives is under the jurisdiction of adults. But for childless adults, it is easier to forget that we are not God. We control when we get up, when we eat, what we do, and when we go to bed. We are the masters of our universe. In Planned Parenthood of Southeastern Pennsylvania v. Casey, the U.S. Supreme Court enshrined Sartre's philosophy as the law of

---

[8] Jean-Paul Sartre, *Existentialism and Human Emotions* (New York: Citadel, 1985), 63.

the land: "At the heart of liberty is the right to define one's own concept of existence, of meaning, of the universe, and of the mystery of human life."[9] In this view, we have a constitutional right to be God.

To some degree, having children brings us back to earth. The desire to be God is thwarted by children. As Michael Sandel points out in his book *Against Perfectionism*,[10] parents do not choose how beautiful, intelligent, athletic, and social their children will be. We get what we get. Parents, unlike an invincible god, are also vulnerable in their children. You might be a multimillionaire, or a celebrity with a gorgeous spouse, but none of that can stop your child from experiencing the normal and sometimes extraordinary pains of life. And as is the case for any good parent, when your child suffers, you also suffer.

It is also impossible to get your children to behave as you would like. What they do—especially as small children and as teenagers—will often be something you wish you could keep them from doing. My wife Jennifer describes one of many such incidents as follows:

> Father Tom had extended a standing invitation to Chris, the little boys, and me to dine with him on Thursday afternoons in the priests' rectory dining room. Thursday was hamburger day. To compensate for the boys' predictably bouncy behavior, I dressed

---

[9] Planned Parenthood of Southeastern Pennsylvania v. Casey (1992), Find-Law, http://caselaw.lp.findlaw.com/scripts/getcase.pl?court=US&vol=505&invol=833.

[10] Michael Sandel, *The Case Against Perfectionism* (Cambridge, Mass.: Belknap, 2009).

them in darling jersey-knit shorts and polo shirts. (Somewhere along the line, we would later discover, George ditched his underpants at a pit stop.) Chris and I spoke sharply to the boys about table manners and inside voices. We positioned ourselves between the boys and cut their hamburgers into bite-size pieces. We brought our own sippy cups. We reminded them to use the potty. Chris even interrupted his meal to take George to the bathroom in spite of his protests that he did not need to go. If only we had listened. He did not need to go—the going having already been done in his darling, loose-fitting jersey shorts. Looking back, of course, we should not have pushed so hard. If we had listened to George's insistence that he did not need to use the restroom, we might have made it out of the dining hall and into the atrium before the pellets began to fall from his shorts. But George was our sixth child, and we knew how embarrassing a public bathroom accident could be. We really enjoyed these afternoons with Father Tom. We did not want to risk losing them. And so Chris excused himself and walked George, through the dining room, to the bathroom. Of course, George did not have to go to the bathroom, and so it was not long before they began their journey back. On the way back, however, Chris noticed a brown, marble-sized ball on the ground and bent down to pick it up lest an elderly priest step on it and take a fall. He was immediately accosted by the smell, immediately determined that it was a little nugget of poop, almost as immediately focused on a trail of little nuggets leading directly from George's chair to the bathroom, and not quite immediately enough raced to pick them all up. Before he could finish, an equally cautious elderly priest had spied a little round nugget and had bent down to pick it up as well. When someone's child is in a serious accident or is suffering with a serious illness, "I'm sorry" is kind but mostly ineffective. When a priest has just laid his bare hand on your child's waste, "I'm sorry" does not even seem kind. The only compensation we could offer was to withdraw ourselves with the alacrity of a gunshot—and, of course, to never return.

Okay, that was embarrassing. But my wife and I have collected a treasure trove of such memories that humble us, mortify us, and make us laugh until we cry. If anything in the world is clear to us parents, it is that we are not God. This realization clears the way to worship the real God.

On the night before Jesus died, he gathered with his apostles for the Last Supper and gave them a new commandment: "A new commandment I give to you, that you love one another; even as I have loved you, that you also love one another" (Jn 13:34). Christians believe that God loves every single human being with an accepting love and a transforming love. God loves each one of us more than we love ourselves and more than words can describe, and he loves us so much that he wants to transform us into his own adoptive children. Good parents love their children in a way similar to how God loves us. They love their children with a love that is unconditional and passionately intense yet of course not at all sexual. Knowing and experiencing something of God's love helps us to love our children as God would.

Finally, let me tell you about what I take to be one of the most frightening passages in the Bible. In Matthew 25:31–46, Jesus describes himself as the Son of man and the King.

> When the Son of man comes in his glory, and all the angels with him, then he will sit on his glorious throne. Before him will be gathered all the nations, and he will separate them one from another as a shepherd separates the sheep from the goats, and he will place the sheep at his right hand, but the goats at the left. Then the King will say to those at his right hand, "Come, O blessed of my Father, inherit the kingdom prepared for you from the foundation of the world; for I was hungry and you gave me food, I was thirsty and you gave me drink, I was a stranger and you welcomed me, I was naked and you clothed me, I was sick and you visited me, I was in prison and you came to me." Then the righteous will answer him, "Lord, when did we see you hungry and feed you, or thirsty and give you drink? And when did we see you a stranger and welcome you, or naked and clothe you? And when did we see you sick or in prison and visit you?" And the King will answer them, "Truly, I say to you, as you did it to one of the least of these my brethren, you did it to me." Then he will say to those at his left hand, "Depart from me, you cursed, into the eternal fire prepared for the devil and his angels; for I was hungry and you gave me no food, I was thirsty and you gave me no drink, I was a stranger and you did not welcome me, naked and you did not clothe me, sick and in prison and you did not visit me." Then they also will answer, "Lord, when did

> we see you hungry or thirsty or a stranger or naked or
> sick or in prison, and did not minister to you?" Then
> he will answer them, "Truly, I say to you, as you did it
> not to one of the least of these, you did it not to me."
> And they will go away into eternal punishment, but the
> righteous into eternal life.

Unless you have been working with Mother Teresa's
Missionaries of Charity, these words may sound frightening. How many of us have ever, let alone on a regular
basis, clothed the naked, fed the hungry, or welcomed the
stranger? I remember hearing this passage as a child, and as
I looked around the church, I thought, practically every-
body here is going to go to hell.

After I had children, I realized that good parents do these
actions every day. Mothers and fathers feed their hungry
children—usually breakfast, lunch, and dinner. They provide drink for the thirsty. Every child invited into a family
is a stranger whom the family gets to know over time.
Parents clothe the naked, first in a literal sense when their
children are babies and then in an extended sense when
they buy their older children clothes. When their children
are sick or in trouble (even in prison), good parents look
after their care. Some people may find a path to heaven by
being good parents.

In this chapter, I have suggested several reasons why
children contribute to the well-being of parents. First,
children are a realization of the drive of erotic love toward
unity. Children both manifest that unity and give rise to
that unity on a physical, social, and emotional level. Second, children aid parents in developing a friendship of virtue by eliciting from the parents repeated good actions that

build up the character of husband and wife. Third, Jesus taught that we must obey the commandments to enter eternal life. Children help their parents to get to heaven by facilitating the parents' obedience to the commandments. How wise of the Second Vatican Council to teach: "Marriage and conjugal love are by their nature ordained toward the procreation and education of children. Children are really the supreme gift of marriage and contribute in the highest degree to their parents' welfare."

The Seventh Big Myth

"All Reproductive Choices Are Equal"

*The Reality: Procreative potential
and bodily union belong together.*

Since human beings have intrinsic dignity and value, the acts of causing new human beings to exist—or the acts preventing them from existing—are ethically significant choices that shape our identities as fundamentally selfish level one and level two people or fundamentally generous level three and level four people. In this chapter, I would like to consider both contraception as well as in vitro fertilization (IVF)—the preventing of human life and the producing of human life. Contraception seeks bodily unity without procreation; IVF seeks procreation without bodily unity.

Contraception

Let us take a look first at contraception. Growing up, I had no clue why anyone would think that contraception was wrong. I was never given any explanation of why the Church teaches what she does. Like most people, as I grew older I thought that contraception was not only perfectly fine but a moral duty in many cases. Only much later did I begin to question what I had been taught by the culture at large.

What exactly is contraception? Contraception is any action that is specifically intended to render the sexual act nonprocreative—whether as an end or as a means.[1] Contraception can be used before sex (for example, the pill), during sex (for example, the condom), or after sex (for example, the morning-after pill) for this nonprocreative purpose.

The question of the morality of contraception hinges in part on the value of procreation of a new human person. From a level one perspective, it is obvious that having a baby does not enhance bodily pleasure; indeed, at least for women, it undermines it. Pregnancies are often taxing and uncomfortable, and pains of giving birth can be fully appreciated by no man. Even for men, however, becoming the father of a baby will likely prove an obstacle, not an enhancement, to the pursuit of bodily pleasure. From a level two perspective, the procreation of children again is unlikely to be accounted worthwhile and valuable. Unless you are the parents of a child movie star, your children will drain your bank account and will hinder your ability to seek fame and fortune, unless you decide to be absent, uninvolved parents. From a level three perspective, having children is quite valuable because procreation makes a new relationship that

[1] This definition comes from Paul VI, *Humanae Vitae,* par. 14, AAS 60 (1968): 490, PE, 277.14.

occasions open-ended, committed service and love of the child. Procreation enhances level three. And at level four, the parents view procreation as a cooperation with God in the creation of a new human being, a person with an eternal destiny. Since from a level three and level four perspective procreation is a great good, to act against procreation—to act "contra conception" (to use contraception)—raises ethical questions.

Indeed, a number of scholars have pointed out that the use of contraception stands in tension with a level three and four identity. They have offered several arguments, including the goods-of-marriage argument, the erotic love argument, the basic human good argument, the sign-of-total-commitment argument, and the integrity argument (referring to the integrity both of the acting person and of the couple). I will say a bit about each.

Saint Augustine of Hippo pointed to faithfulness, love, and children as the goods of marriage.[2] That faithfulness is good for a marriage is obvious. Committing adultery hinders the good of fidelity in marriage, so virtuous people do not commit adultery. Love is another obvious good of marriage, so loving people do not do acts of hatred against their spouse. The procreation of children too, as we talked about in the previous chapter, is a good of marriage. And the point of contraception is to act against the conception of a new human person. Contraception seeks to remove a great good, the good of procreation. So if couples with a friendship of virtue seek the good for one another and do

---

[2] Augustine, *De bono coniugali; De sancta virginitate* (Oxford: Oxford University Press, 2013).

not act against the good, then married friends of virtue do not use contraception.

Alexander Pruss, in his wonderful book *One Body: An Essay in Christian Sexual Ethics*, presents an argument from erotic love against the use of contraception.[3] In chapter 1, we described erotic love as the desire for comprehensive union with the beloved. Erotic love involves accepting and appreciating the whole person. When you are in love with another person, you love not just an attractive body but that person's personality, quirks, and singularity as a person. By contrast, mere sexual attraction delights in a person only under a limited description, as a sexual partner (or a potential sexual partner). In love you find the person so lovable that you desire a comprehensive union with the beloved. However, to choose to contracept is to reject full union with the beloved, since the beloved's bodily dimension of fertility is not accepted. Instead, an important aspect of the person is viewed as defective and in need of correction, namely, the person's procreative power, the potential to become a father or a mother with you. Contraception involves not loving and accepting the whole person, because the beloved's procreative power is specifically undermined.

Germain Grisez and his colleagues offer another argument against contraception, the basic human good argument.[4] Generous people do not act against basic human goods, such as human life, intelligence, and friendship. To kill an innocent person intentionally, to give someone a

[3] Alexander Pruss, *One Body: An Essay in Christian Sexual Ethics* (Notre Dame, Ind.: University of Notre Dame Press, 2013), 272–74.

[4] Germain Grisez, Joseph Boyle, John Finnis, and William E. May, " 'Every Marital Act Ought to Be Open to New Life': Toward a Clearer Understanding", *Thomist* 52 (1988): 365–426.

lobotomy in order to destroy intelligence, and to destroy someone's friendship deliberately are all actions that a generous person does not do because altruists seek to love other people, and love for others seeks the good of others rather than evil for others. As we noted in the previous chapter, procreation is a basic human good. Now, the use of contraception is aimed against the good of procreation, since the one using contraception aims to render a procreative act nonprocreative. If virtuous people never act against a basic human good, and contraception acts against procreation, then virtuous people do not use contraception.

Another argument given against the use of contraception is the sign-of-total-commitment argument.[5] In the marital vows, as we saw previously, the husband gives himself as a spouse totally to his wife, and vice versa. This verbal language of self-giving is mirrored by the body language of self-giving found in the act of sexual intercourse. Marital acts, in other words, at least implicitly reaffirm the marital vows. Just as the marital vows indicate a total spousal gift of self, so too marital acts should reflect this total gift of self. The use of contraception is not a total gift of self, since openness to being a mother or a father is deliberately withheld from the spouse. Openness to life is a sign of total commitment, a commitment so real that both spouses are open to having a permanent embodiment of that union emerge nine months later.

A final argument against the use of contraception is the integrity argument.[6] Personal integrity and self-harmony,

---

[5] John F. Kippley, *Sex and the Marriage Covenant: A Basis for Morality*, 2nd ed. (San Francisco: Ignatius Press, 2005).

[6] Pruss, *One Body*, 274–76.

a unity of one's body and one's conscious self, is a good. For instance, when a person lies to another person, the liar introduces a disharmony within himself. His body expresses one thing ("I didn't take the money"), but his mind holds to another thing ("I did take the money"). In sexual intercourse, the bodies of the couple strive for procreation. The man's body strives to emit sperm so as to impregnate the woman; her body strives to receive sperm so as to be impregnated. The use of contraception, however, sets the conscious will of the person against the bodily striving of the person. So contraception involves a lack of personal integrity and self-harmony, intentionally bringing about a disharmony between body and will. A similar disharmony is produced in the couple. A couple have the interpersonal good of integrity and harmony when they work together rather than set themselves at cross-purposes. Pruss puts the point as follows:

> The person's body is striving for reproduction. But on a voluntary level, the person is actively set against it. Thus the biological striving is not reflective of the person as a whole. On the contrary, the person as a whole is crucially disunited from the body. But if in the sexual act the two persons are supposed to be united *through* their bodies, then in being disunited from their bodies, the persons are thereby disunited from each other. Hence the deliberately contracepted sexual act fails to unite the persons as persons, since it disunites the persons from the act by which they are supposed to be united.[7]

If one or both persons are using contraceptives, the couple undermine the integrity of their unity as persons because

[7] Ibid., 275.

the choice to contracept sets one partner against the other partner's bodily striving.

Some people think that if they do not use contraception, then they will have eighteen children and be completely overwhelmed. They believe that contraception is necessary to preserve marital harmony and sanity. I can certainly understand that there are circumstances in which having a child, or having another child, would bring incredible difficulty. I was in such circumstances myself. During graduate school at the University of Notre Dame, my salary was ten thousand dollars a year. My family had no health insurance, and the oldest of our three children was not yet four years old. Jennifer recounts:

Our monthly rent was $125. This was excellent news. But, of course, though people like to joke about graduate school being a time of suspended reality, the principles of economics are never suspended. In grad school, as in life, you get what you pay for. We soon discovered that our money secured us a mere five hundred square feet of real estate, all of which, to my horror, was subterranean. I also discovered that I could vacuum our entire apartment from one outlet. It was both appalling and, considering we had no money whatsoever, appealing. Fights were common—and sometimes unwittingly public. One winter day, in an effort to show how mature we were, my husband and I offered to babysit for our next-door neighbors. "Go out!" we encouraged. "Enjoy some time together," we said, feeling terribly magnanimous. I don't remember how it started, or what it was about, but less than an hour before we were to be entrusted with this couple's children, Chris and I had one of the biggest, loudest, most grievous fights we'd ever had. We stood toe-to-toe in our kitchen screaming at each other until the phone rang. "Hi," began Mark from next door, in a voice that clearly said: "Don't mind me. Your marriage is your business, but these walls are terribly thin." "Listen," he actually said, "Claire and I have decided to stay in tonight, but, hey, thanks for the offer." We didn't leave the apartment for a week.[8]

Not just because of marital strife but also due to our relative poverty and lack of space, we did not think that adding a fourth baby to the mix was a good idea. Many people think that the only alternatives for couples such as us are contraception or complete abstinence, but there is a third way.

Natural family planning (NFP) and fertility awareness methods (FAMs) are ways of either achieving pregnancy or avoiding pregnancy that rely on an understanding of when a woman ovulates and then timing sexual intercourse accordingly. There are a number of ways to determine when ovulation takes place, and these methods are highly reliable when used properly. According to a press release from the European Society for Human Reproduction and Embryology, "Researchers have found that a method of

---

[8] Modified from Jennifer Kaczor, "It Takes a University Village", *Notre Dame Magazine*, Summer 2012, http://magazine.nd.edu/news/31401-echoes-it-takes-a-university-village/.

natural family planning that uses two indicators to identify the fertile phase in a woman's menstrual cycle is as effective as the contraceptive pill for avoiding unplanned pregnancies if used correctly, according to a report published online in Europe's leading reproductive medicine journal *Human Reproduction*."[9] Unlike the contraceptive pill, NFP and FAMs are inexpensive, healthy, and natural.

Now, some people think that NFP and FAMs are simply other kinds of contraception. It is true that NFP and FAMs can be used with the same motivation—to avoid pregnancy. Yet in evaluating an action morally, not just the motive but also the means chosen are relevant. Nothing is wrong with the motive of making money for your family, but the means of honest work and the means of theft are not morally equivalent, despite their shared motivation.

So are NFP and FAMs simply other forms of contraception? As we saw earlier, contraception is any action that before, during, or after sexual intercourse is specifically intended to render the sexual act infertile, whether as an end or as a means. But NFP and FAMs do nothing that before, during, or after sexual intercourse is specifically intended to render the sexual act nonprocreative, whether as an end or as a means. Couples using NFP or FAMs, if they wish to avoid pregnancy, simply abstain temporarily from sexual acts. Since they are not doing sexual acts during times of abstention, the couple cannot be rendering these nonexistent sexual acts nonprocreative.

[9]European Society for Human Reproduction and Embryology, "Natural Family Planning Method as Effective as Contraceptive Pill, New Research Finds", *Science Daily*, February 21, 2007, http://www.sciencedaily.com/releases /2007/02/070221065200.htm.

Clearly, abstaining—either temporarily or permanently—cannot be a form of contraception. If abstaining were a form of contraception, then everyone who abstains from sex would be using contraception—babies, celibate nuns, great-grandmas, and the pope included. So NFP and FAMs are not contraception.

Some people point to the case of rape as one in which preventing birth is justified—and they are right. But such cases are not contraception in the morally relevant sense. Germain Grisez explains:

> Rape is the imposition of intimate, bodily union upon someone without her or his consent, and anyone who is raped rightly resists so far as possible. Moreover, the victim (or potential victim) is right to resist not only insofar as he or she is subjected to unjust force, but insofar as that force imposes the special wrong of uniquely intimate bodily contact. It can scarcely be doubted that someone who cannot prevent the initiation of this intimacy is morally justified in resisting its continuation; for example, a woman who awakes and finds herself being penetrated by a rapist need not permit her attacker to ejaculate in her vagina if she can make him withdraw. On the same basis, if they cannot prevent the wrongful intimacy itself, women who are victims (or potential victims) of rape and those trying to help them are morally justified in trying to prevent conception insofar as it is the fullness of sexual union. The measures taken in this case are a defense of the woman's ovum (insofar as it is a part of her person) against the rapist's sperms (insofar as they are parts of his person). By contrast, if the intimate, bodily union of intercourse is not imposed on the woman but sought or willingly permitted, neither she nor anyone who

permits the union can intend at the same time that it not occur. Hence, rape apart, contraceptive measures are chosen to prevent conception not insofar as it is the ultimate completion of intimate bodily union but insofar as it is the beginning of a new and unwanted person.[10]

When a woman is raped, she does not choose to perform a sexual act, because rape by definition involves a lack of consent. Rather, in getting raped, she is acted against, contrary to her consent. Since the act is not a voluntary act (as far as she is concerned), the rape is not *her* sexual act. If she does not perform a sexual act, then she also cannot be contracepting in the morally relevant sense; she is not rendering *her* sexual act nonprocreative. In a similar sense, a nun who takes medication to regulate her menstrual cycles is not using contraception, even if other women take the exact same prescription for the purposes of contraception; since the nun is not choosing to do sexual acts, her action in taking the pill is not contraception.

The Problem of Infertility

The desire of a married couple to have a child is a natural and normal outgrowth of their erotic love for each other. The two sought a deeper unity by forming the comprehensive union that is their marriage, and the fruit of that organic union of living human bodies is another living human body, their son or daughter. Unfortunately,

[10] Germain Grisez, *Living a Christian Life*, vol. 2 of *The Way of the Lord Jesus* (Quincy, Ill.: Franciscan Press, 1993), chap. 8, question E. Also available online at http://twotlj.org.

many couples suffer from infertility problems, so this manifestation is made more difficult to achieve. We will now talk about some possible responses to fertility problems and how these problems should be approached by the kind of people who seek level three and level four happiness.

Many people believe that infertility is mostly a female problem, but in fact roughly equal numbers of men and women struggle with it. Many people—6.1 million Americans alone, about 10 percent of all people of reproductive age—suffer from infertility. It is true, however, that there are important differences between men and women in terms of reproduction. Men can, in principle, become fathers at any stage of life. Women, by contrast, have a limited window of fertility. Unfortunately, many women do not realize just how limited this window really is. Miriam Grossman, in her book *Unprotected: A Campus Psychiatrist Reveals How Political Correctness in Her Profession Endangers Every Student*, draws on her experience counseling students, both graduate and undergraduate, at the University of California at Los Angeles. She tells the story of "Amanda", a thirty-nine-year-old woman who earned a doctorate, had a prestigious position, and yet also yearned to have a family of her own. In comparison to when she was thirty, her likelihood of having a baby had decreased by some 75 percent. The possibility that she would conceive but then miscarry had tripled, the likelihood of the baby being stillborn had doubled, and the chance that the baby would have a genetic abnormality was six times as great as it was when she was 30. Her baby, if she conceived, would be more likely to be premature, underweight, and mentally and physically disabled.[11]

Despite Amanda's sophisticated understanding of so many matters, her sexual education did not emphasize these fertility facts. Her sexual education, both formally in school and informally via *Cosmopolitan*, focused almost exclusively on how *not* to get pregnant, as if achieving pregnancy were never a problem. Amanda had a vague idea of the ticking of her biological clock, but she simply did not know how quickly the window of healthy fertility closes. The reality of declining fertility was taking place, but she was not educated enough about it to make an informed decision about when to marry and to try to have a baby. As Mark Regnerus and Jeremy Uecker note, "It's a biological reality that women's fertility plateaus at age 20 and stays there for less than 10 years before beginning its slow decline just prior to age 30 (and then a more rapid decline around age 35)."[12] What Amanda did not know did hurt her, as she approached forty and wrapped her mind around the very likely possibility that she would never be a mother and that no child would ever call her "Grandma". If a woman delays marriage until her thirties and then does not begin to try to have children for a few years, the likelihood of her giving birth is greatly lessened. Add to this the STIs that hinder fertility for many couples, and the situation becomes desperate for those who want a baby.

[11] Miriam Grossman, *Unprotected: A Campus Psychiatrist Reveals How Political Correctness in Her Profession Endangers Every Student* (New York: Sentinel, 2007), 120–21.

[12] Mark Regnerus and Jeremy Uecker, *Premarital Sex in America: How Young Americans Meet, Mate, and Think about Marrying* (New York: Oxford University Press, 2011), 186.

Making Babies without Making Love: IVF

What can Amanda do if she and her husband want to have a baby but struggle with fertility problems? Some couples in this position opt for In Vitro Fertilization (IVF). IVF is a process of combining human egg and sperm (either from the couple themselves or from donors) in order to make human embryos in a laboratory, some of which are implanted in the uterus. Each round of IVF costs on average $12,400, which is usually not covered by health insurance. This out-of-pocket expense makes IVF a very expensive option, particularly in light of the relatively low rate of success—only 29.4 percent of IVF users experience the success of live birth in any particular round. Nevertheless, since IVF was first introduced in 1978, there have been more than 114,000 babies in the United States born as a result of the technique. Still, less than 5 percent of infertile couples turn to IVF for help.

Would an altruistic, virtuous person use IVF? Is it something that someone seeking level three and level four happiness ought to make use of? Amanda herself did not see any particular difficulty whatsoever with the reproductive technology, but certain cases troubled her.

Many people agree to the modest thesis that reproductive technology can be misused. Perhaps the poster child of IVF gone wild is Nadya Suleman, the "Octomom". Although she already had six IVF children, the oldest of whom was age seven, Suleman gave birth to eight more babies conceived through IVF on January 26, 2009. At the time, Suleman was unmarried, unemployed, and on public-assistance programs. Both Suleman and her doctor were roundly condemned for the injustice of their actions.

It is not fair to the children or to the public to create off-spring that one is unable to care for properly. As noted in an earlier chapter, single parenthood endangers the well-being of children, so from a level three and a level four perspective, children should not be conceived unless they can be raised by married parents.

But let us change the Suleman case a bit. Let us say that IVF is used by a married couple who are able to care for their own children. Is it ethical for them to use IVF?

The couple's desire to have a child together is noble and understandable. But at issue is not simply having a baby but the means by which a baby is made. Is IVF a good means, or is it ethically problematic? IVF can make use of the couple's own gametes, their own sperm and eggs (homologous IVF), or it can make use of a donor's sperm or eggs (heterologous IVF). We will start with the question of donor gametes.

Heterologous IVF is ethically problematic in part because of what takes place before the sperm and eggs are combined—both for the gamete donor and for the children conceived. Heterologous IVF presupposes egg donation. A documentary called *Eggsploitation* explores the dangers of egg donation for young women who are lured into either giving their eggs away or selling their eggs.[13] The health risks of induced ovarian hyperstimulation, by which many eggs are collected, range from the mild and irritating, such as abrupt weight gain and shortness of breath, to the potentially deadly, such as blood clots and kidney failure. The long-term health risks of hyperstimulation of the ovaries is unknown.

[13] Center for Bioethics and Culture, *Eggsploitation* (San Ramon, Calif.: Center for Bioethics and Culture Network, 2010).

By contrast, sperm donation does not subject a man to health risks. However, it does subject a man to becoming a biological father of an unknown number of children. This is deeply irresponsible, for in donating his sperm, a man cannot in any way take responsibility for his own biological children, nor can he raise them properly since he does not even know them. He cannot ensure to the best of his ability that these children have a good mother. Years later, his own biological children might even marry one other, or even marry him since he (and they) would not know their incestuous biological relationship.

Alexander Pruss, in *One Body*, makes the point that anonymous gamete donation is deeply irresponsible. If you are a parent, ask yourself what percentage of people you would trust to raise and educate your own children about moral and religious matters. If you are not a parent, imagine having children, and then ask yourself the same question. Pruss writes:

> If you live in the United States, then no matter what your religious affiliation (counting lack of religion as an affiliation), the likelihood that a recipient couple will provide them [your children] with the kind of religious education (if any) of which you approve is less than fifty percent. But given the centrality to life of religion, getting religious education right (and of course some may think this means not providing any religious education and simply letting the child choose, and some may think this means providing an atheistic education) is an important part of parental responsibilities.... Once one adds moral and academic education to the mix, you will surely have to think the likelihood to be slim that a couple chosen by the clinic will provide the right kind of education for your child.[14]

To donate gametes to a clinic is therefore incompatible with parental responsibilities for the upbringing and education of the resulting children.

Anonymous gamete donation carries with it special burdens for the children, who will never know their father or their mother—or both. A report released internationally by the Commission on Parenthood's Future, *My Daddy's Name Is Donor: A New Study of Young Adults Conceived through Sperm Donation*, notes, "Young adults conceived through sperm donation (or 'donor offspring') experience profound struggles with their origins and identities.... Donor offspring are significantly more likely than those raised by their biological parents to struggle with serious, negative outcomes such as delinquency, substance abuse, and depression, even when controlling for socio-economic and other factors."[15] Lindsay Greenawalt, on her blog *Confessions of a Cryokid*, expresses her anguish: "If I had to choose between being conceived with half of my identity and half of my kinship deliberately denied from me for eternity—or never being born—I'd choose never being born." She continued, "We were created to carry a loss. A loss that no human being should have to endure."[16]

Making use of donor eggs or sperm is also deeply problematic for several other reasons for those seeking level

---

[14] Pruss, *One Body*, 387.

[15] Elizabeth Marquardt, Norval D. Glenn, and Karen Clark, *My Daddy's Name Is Donor: A New Study of Young Adults Conceived through Sperm Donation* (New York: Broadway, 2010), 7, 9.

[16] Lindsay Greenawalt, "Happy Thanksgiving ... Oh Yeah, and Be Grateful to Have Been Born", *Confessions of a Cryokid* (blog), November 26, 2009, http://cryokidconfessions.blogspot.com/2009/11/happy-thanksgivingoh-yeah-and-be.html.

three and level four happiness.[17] The first is that marriage is a comprehensive union, a living, exclusive "you alone", an indissoluble "forever" bond. The fruit of this union ought to reflect what this union is. It is wrong to act against this exclusivity by performing acts that should be reserved for spouses. To have sex with a person who is not one's spouse or to reproduce a child with a person who is not one's spouse contradicts the exclusivity of marriage. Rather than the child being made by the husband and wife alone, some extramarital third party (the egg donor) or fourth party (the sperm donor) intervenes. Since heterologous IVF reproduces a child with a person who is not one's spouse by using either sperm or eggs that are not from one's spouse, heterologous IVF is contrary to the nature of marriage as a comprehensive union. Just as a couple should not seek the unitive dimension of marriage divorced from the procreative—as happens with the use of contraception—so too they ought not to seek the procreative dimension divorced from the unitive. There can be no true unity if an aspect of the beloved—namely, the procreative possibility of being a father or a mother with the spouse—is rejected. So too the procreative good is compromised when achieved without a real unity of the persons procreating.

A second reason why virtuous people do not knowingly and willingly use heterologous IVF is that children have a right to an integral identity. If a child has one

---

[17] Here I expand a bit on three arguments put forward in Congregation for the Doctrine of the Faith, *Donum Vitae: Instruction on Respect for Human Life in Its Origin and on the Dignity of Procreation; Replies to Certain Questions of the Day* (Vatican City: Libreria Editrice Vaticana, 1987), section 1.

set of biological parents (the gamete donors), and a different woman as a gestational mother, and a third set of adoptive parents who raise the child, then this child has been deprived of an integral identity. This "diffusion" of parental identity and the concomitant diffusion of parental responsibility deprive the child of something to which he was entitled to. Many times, children conceived through heterologous IVF deeply desire to know who their biological father or mother is. The dignity and vulnerability of each child entail a responsibility for those who procreate to do so within marriage, with each other alone as a couple.

Turning now away from the use of donor gametes and to homologous IVF, in which the husband's and wife's gametes are used, is IVF in these circumstances ethically acceptable? I would answer that there are serious problems with IVF even if no donor gametes are used. I say this for several reasons, the first of which is that IVF endangers the well-being of oneself or another without a serious reason. Let me explain.

Even those who are advocates of IVF recognize that it endangers the well-being of women. Ronald Green has noted the "enormous frustration" of women with IVF, and the fact that "homes have been mortgaged to pay tens of thousands of dollars" for this procedure, which more often than not results in no live birth.[18] He notes, "Each year thousands of women are subjected to powerful drugs with unknown consequences for long-term health [risks, including] risk of cancer."[19] Tarek A. Gelbaya, in the 2010

[18] Ronald Green, *The Human Embryo Research Debates: Bioethics in the Vortex of Controversy* (Oxford: Oxford University Press, 2001), 2.

[19] Ibid., 15, 81.

article "Short and Long-Term Risks to Women Who Conceive through In Vitro Fertilization", notes the legion of problems that women using IVF face, including ovarian hyperstimulation syndrome, increased levels of anxiety and depression, ovarian torsion, ectopic pregnancy, preeclampsia, placenta previa, placental separation, increased risk of cesarean section, and, most seriously, multiple pregnancy.[20] IVF kills women each year in two ways: through ovarian hyperstimulation syndrome, in which ovaries swell and leak fluid into the body cavity, and through complications from multiple pregnancy.

Aside from the serious risks to the mother, the child also is endangered in several ways. U.S. fertility labs typically create around twenty-four human embryos and then implant only two or three in utero. This process leaves more than twenty human embryos in a state of limbo. They are often frozen for future use, sometimes donated for lethal embryonic research, or just discarded. As of 2012, there were around four hundred thousand frozen "spare" embryos in the United States. I use the term "spare" with reservation and only because the term has become so common. No human being should be treated like a spare, akin to a spare tire, to be used if it suits the purposes of others. From a level three and a level four perspective, all human beings—regardless of race, size, religion, age, dependency, or health condition—are entitled to respect and treatment as persons with dignity. To freeze them, discard them, or leave them as "spares" is to violate human dignity.

---

[20] Tarek A. Gelbaya, "Short and Long-Term Risks to Women Who Conceive through In Vitro Fertilization", *Human Fertility* 13, no. 1 (2010): 19–27.

Not only is the dignity of the so-called spare human embryos compromised, but often the well-being of the "select" human embryos is also compromised. After the select embryos are implanted in the woman's uterus, the well-being and human dignity of the developing sons or daughters is violated through what is called "selective reduction", by which a multiple pregnancy—say, four babies—is reduced to twins.

It is possible to perform IVF in such a way that the aforementioned difficulties are avoided, although in the United States this is rarely done. The parents could use their own gametes rather than donor gametes. They could create and implant just one or two embryos. This scenario alleviates both the concern for unimplanted embryos as well as the objection to fetal reduction. But even in this case, an ethical problem remains because IVF children who "make it" to birth have an increased risk of serious problems. One study found that

> babies born via in vitro fertilization (IVF) treatment are at higher risk of developing cancer at childhood, researchers reveal. The study published in the journal *Fertility and Sterility* found that fertility treatments increased the risk of childhood cancer by 33 percent.[21]

Another study found that "infants conceived with use of intracytoplasmic sperm injection or in vitro fertilization have twice as high a risk of a major birth defect as

[21] Roshni Mahesh, "IVF Babies at Higher Risk of Childhood Cancer: Study", *International Business Times* (October 8, 2013). Available at http://www.ibtimes.co.in/articles/512225/20131008/ivf-treatment-infertility-childhood-cancer-leukaemia.htm.

naturally conceived infants."[22] These troubling outcomes are confirmed by a Swedish study that noted increased risk of cerebral paralysis and birth defects for IVF children.[23] Carlo Bellieni, professor of neonatal therapy at the School of Pediatrics of the University of Siena, notes,

> In the case of the conception of a single child, the rate of risk for his health, if born by in vitro fertilization, is greater than for the normal population. A recent analysis of 25 scientific studies published in the *British Medical Journal* concludes that single pregnancies from assisted reproduction have a significantly worse perinatal result in relation to the normal population, although it adds that in twin pregnancies, perinatal mortality is about 40% lower after IVF in comparison with natural conception.[24]

The risk of having a handicapped child by opting for IVF is 11 percent, compared with 5 percent by normal conception, so IVF endangers the well-being of human beings by significantly increasing the likelihood of serious illness.

Is there a serious reason for risking these effects? Is the desire to become a biological parent a serious reason? I am not sure that it is. From a level two perspective, one can

[22] M. Hansen, J. J. Kurinczuk, C. Bower, and S. Webb, "The Risk of Major Birth Defects after Intracytoplasmic Sperm Injection and In Vitro Fertilization", *New England Journal of Medicine* 346, no. 10 (2002): 725.

[23] Gideon Koren, "Adverse Effects of Assisted Reproductive Technology and Pregnancy Outcome", *Pediatric Research* (2002): 136.

[24] See the interview "In Vitro Children and the Risks They Face", in which Bellieni cites Frans M. Helmerhorst, D. A. Perquin, D. Donker, and M. J. Keirse, "Perinatal Outcome of Singletons and Twins after Assisted Conception: A Systematic Review of Controlled Studies", *British Medical Journal* 328 (2004): 261. Interview available from Zenit, June 6, 2004, http://www.zenit. org/article-10293?l=english.

see a kind of ego boost from having one's own biological child. It might be an added pleasure to see how much a child looks like oneself or acts like oneself. In terms of level three, however, an adoptive parent and a biological parent can both provide loving care for a child. Unfortunately, there are children without parents already, so parents who adopt make a lifetime contribution to the well-being of these already-existing children.

I am not sure even if adopting a child versus conceiving one biologically makes much of a difference to the parents in terms of their day-to-day living. Do parents with both adopted and biological children feel a difference between them? In my own case, my father told me that there were years at a time when the fact of my adoption never even entered his mind. I was his son, period. I was not his son in some qualified, unreal sense; I was not his "adopted" son. I was—and am—his son.

Some people believe that it is permissible to use IVF because they have a right to have a baby. Strictly speaking, this is false. A person can have a right to property, but a person does not have a right to possess another human being, even if it is one's own baby. Married couples do have a right to perform acts of a procreative kind—in other words, nothing is wrong with them performing acts apt for generation—but a right to engage in acts of a reproductive kind is something different from a right actually to have a baby. Similarly, a natural-born U.S. citizen thirty-five years of age or older has the right to run for president of the United States, but he has no right to *be* president, as if all failed presidential candidates have had their rights violated.

From a level four perspective, speaking about a "right to a child" is misplaced. A child is always a gift to be given freely by one spouse to another in cooperation with God. The language of "right to a child" misconstrues and distorts the reality of children as gifts.

William May, in his book *Marriage: The Rock on Which the Family Is Built*,[25] offers another argument against IVF. Generating a human being in a laboratory is a form of production, the making of a product. But a human person is not a product, so he should not be treated as a thing or a product. This principle is clearly enunciated by Immanuel Kant's categorical imperative that humanity, whether one's own person or the person of another, should never be used simply as a means but should always be respected as an end in itself. And if a human being is always to be treated as a person rather than as a product or a thing, then he should also not be generated as if he were a thing or a product. But in IVF this is precisely what takes place—the production of human beings.

Janet Smith and I, in a book called *Life Issues, Medical Choices*,[26] develop another argument against IVF, including homologous IVF, in which the gametes are given by the husband and wife. Some actions may not be delegated to others, such as writing love letters or taking out a spouse for a twenty-fifth anniversary dinner. It would be wrong to "farm out" such tasks to another, even if that other person were a better writer or could afford a better dinner. In marriage, spouses may not delegate to others the mutual and exclusive exchange of persons with respect to

[25] William May, *Marriage: The Rock on Which the Family Is Built* (San Francisco, Ignatius Press, 2009).

[26] Janet E. Smith and Christopher Kaczor, *Life Issues, Medical Choices* (Cincinnati, Oh.: Servant, 2007).

reproductive acts. They cannot delegate to others the right to engage in the marital act (even if one spouse cannot make love) or the right to procreate (even if one spouse is infertile). In IVF, it is the laboratory technicians who produce the baby rather than the husband and wife.

If IVF is wrong, what about the children conceived through IVF? Are we saying that these human beings should not exist? Hundreds of thousands of human beings, perhaps some of them reading this book, were conceived in this way. Isn't the world a better place because they exist?

All human beings, regardless of how, when, why, and by whom they were conceived, have equal human dignity.[27] It does not matter whether they were conceived through IVF or not. They may have been conceived by a husband and wife deeply in love and both desiring to conceive a child on their wedding anniversary. They may have been conceived by a couple who did not know each other and desperately wanted to avoid pregnancy. The circumstances of their conception do not in the least call into question the equal basic moral worth of all human beings.

However, although all human beings have equal basic moral worth, not all ways of conceiving children are equally moral. Many children have been conceived by adultery, incest, or rape, which are obviously immoral acts. As I argued earlier, sex outside of marriage is morally impermissible, and although I was conceived by this kind of act myself, my human dignity is no less than any other person's. Children conceived through IVF have the same basic dignity as everyone else, but it does not follow

[27] See Christopher Kaczor, *The Ethics of Abortion: Women's Rights, Human Life, and the Question of Justice* (New York: Routledge, 2011).

from this that IVF is morally right. Precisely because of the innate worth of all human beings, they should be conceived in ways that respect their dignity.

An Alternative to IVF: NaProTechnology

So if a couple struggle with infertility, what can they do? An infertility solution better than IVF is to be found in NaProTechnology. Medical doctor Thomas Hilgers spent decades looking into individual causes of infertility as well as developing specialized treatments for the various pathologies that block normal human reproduction. His findings are presented in his book *The Medical and Surgical Practice of NaProTechnology*.[28] By treating the pathologies that interfere with fertility, Hilgers has a method of helping infertile couples that has proven tremendously successful. The rate of success for NaProTechnology is up to 80 percent, compared with 29 percent for IVF. The expense is also much less than IVF and is typically covered by health insurance. Best of all, NaProTechnology has none of the ethical difficulties of IVF—it does not use donor gametes, it does not endanger the well-being of the humans conceived, and it does not delegate to others the making of the baby.

Love, marriage, and baby carriage—the traditional triplet fit well together. That is why infertility is such a trial and a cross for so many couples. We are fortunate in the twenty-first century to have so many ways to restore and promote fertility so that ever more couples can enjoy the blessings of a baby.

[28] Thomas Hilgers, *The Medical and Surgical Practice of NaProTechnology* (Omaha, Neb.: Pope Paul VI Institute Press, 2004).

EPILOGUE

I would like to conclude with a brief word about the role of religion in a marriage. Although happily married couples can live with irreconcilable differences, people contemplating marriage should still seek out a spouse with as few such differences as possible. And there is one difference that it is especially important to highlight—religious differences. I learned from empirical research on marriage that shared faith is very important for married couples. All couples have irreconcilable differences of some kind, but when a couple share a religious faith, their likelihood of divorce is lower than that of couples who do not share a faith. "Among mixed marriages, Catholics who marry Protestants or non-religious spouses have a divorce rate of 49% and 48% respectively. Catholics who marry someone of an "other" non-Protestant religion, such as Judaism, have a 35% rate, while Catholics who marry Catholics have a 27% divorce rate."[1] Even more important is the *practice* of religious faith, which lowers the likelihood of divorce still further. I know in my own case that my wife and I sharing Catholic faith has helped us through difficult

[1] Wayne Laugesen, "Divorce Statistics Indicate Catholic Couples Are Less Likely to Break Up", *National Catholic Register*, 11/14/2013, http://www.ncregister.com/daily-news/divorce-statistics-indicate-catholic-couples-are-less-likely-to-break-up/.

times—as well as led to deeper shared enjoyment of the best of times.

Since marriage aims at the deeper levels of happiness, it is more than fitting to end this discussion by mentioning a great joy that came from marriage. This joy was made even more delightful since my wife and I share Catholic faith.

In 2013, our daughter received her First Holy Communion. It was also a last First Communion because all my other children have passed beyond this most lovely of markers. If there is anything more beautiful than First Holy Communion, I have not yet encountered it. First Communion is so pure, so innocent, and so wonderful. The boys look spiffed up in black pants and white ties; the girls in their white dresses foreshadow distant weddings. The whole family is present—Mom, Dad, siblings, grandparents, and other relatives. The color white, the liturgical color for the Easter season, still adorns the environment. And in my parish, Saint Anastasia in Westchester, California, each First Communion family makes a banner that hangs in the church. My wife has worked over the years to add extra "bling" to ours with each child.

The ceremony is custom-made to tug at the heart and to call to mind God's great gifts—family, Church, sacraments. At the center of attention is the child receiving Holy Communion. These second-grade children are big enough to understand that the Host is not just a symbol but really is the Body, Blood, soul, and divinity of Christ. At the same time, these children are little enough to speak with childish lisps and to have the wonder and the frolic of toddlers. Second-graders enjoy a wonderful age, with all its distinctive charm, perched square between adulthood and babyhood.

First Holy Communion naturally brings to mind the whole arch of a human life. At such times, we remember the birth of the child, the baptism, and the first day of school. At such times, we look forward to graduations, weddings, and the birth of grandchildren. At such times too, it is hard not to be overwhelmed with the generosity of God. It is hard even to be aware, let alone count, all that God has done for us. God gave us this child, protected and fostered the child's growth, and now draws the child closer to himself, indeed unites the child with himself in the Blessed Sacrament. The innocence, purity, and beauty of each child unite with the perfect innocence, purity, and beauty of God.

During the First Communion Mass at Saint Anastasia, each child comes forward with his parents to receive for the very first time. Mom, Dad, and God cooperated in making the child; Mom, Dad, and God cooperated in baptizing the child; and now Mom, Dad, and God are together as the child receives First Holy Communion.

After Mass is over, the children, the priests, and those who prepared them gather on the back steps of the church for a group photo as the cars on Manchester Boulevard slow down to see. Drivers passing by honk and give the thumbs-up sign, some perhaps recalling their own First Communion. Then our family returns home to celebrate together with grandparents, relatives, and friends. Photos are taken, rosaries received, food consumed.

This First Communion was the last time I will ever get to experience this delightful passage, and it was an experience to be savored. We all need these small foretastes of heaven.